Textual Patterns

Key words and corpus analysis in language education

Mike Scott

University of Liverpool

Christopher Tribble

King's College, London University

John Benjamins Publishing Company

Amsterdam / Philadelphia

™ The paper used in this publication meets the minimum requirements
of American National Standard for Information Sciences – Permanence
of Paper for Printed Library Materials, ANSI z39.48-1984.

Cover illustration from original painting *Random Order*
by Lorenzo Pezzatini, Florence, 1996.

Library of Congress Cataloging-in-Publication Data

Mike Scott
    Textual Patterns : Key words and corpus analysis in language education /
        Mike Scott and Christopher Tribble.
        p. cm. (Studies in Corpus Linguistics, ISSN 1388–0373 ; v. 22)
    Includes bibliographical references and indexes.
        1. language and languages--Computer-assisted instruction. 2.
    Discourse analysis--Data processing--Study and teaching. I. Tribble, Chris.
    II. Title. III. Series.

    P53.28.S37 2006
    418.00285--dc22   2006040658
    ISBN 90 272 2293 2 (Hb; alk. paper)
    ISBN 90 272 2294 0 (Pb; alk. paper)

John Benjamins Publishing Co. · P.O. Box 36224 · 1020 ME Amsterdam · The Netherlands
John Benjamins North America · P.O. Box 27519 · Philadelphia PA 19118-0519 · USA

Table of contents

Textual Patterns

Studies in Corpus Linguistics

SCL focuses on the use of corpora throughout language study, the development of a quantitative approach to linguistics, the design and use of new tools for processing language texts, and the theoretical implications of a data-rich discipline.

General Editor

Elena Tognini-Bonelli

Consulting Editor

Wolfgang Teubert

Volume 22

Textual Patterns: Key words and corpus analysis in language education
by Mike Scott and Christopher Tribble

Preface

This volume is divided into two major sections, the first being more resource and theory-based, the second largely applied to a set of distinct areas of knowledge. In the first, in Chapters 1 to 5, Mike Scott introduces and explains software resources which are relevant to those undertaking corpus-based research or teaching preparation, and some problematic aspects of the underlying theories. These are illustrated with a series of studies. In Part 2 Chris Tribble has written a series of research articles which provide further examples of how language teachers and researchers can draw on these approaches to develop pedagogically valuable insights into language in use.

Scott's section starts off with a chapter which does not involve any studies but questions and theories. Chapter 1 therefore considers some of the characteristics of corpus-based research, in terms of a quest for underlying pattern. Throughout the book we are identifying patterns in text. There are also four different starting-points for the corpus-based researcher, the text, the language, the culture, the brain. Finally there is the question of scope: what sort of context are we dealing with? The amount of text within the researcher's scope can go from the smallest context up to the whole text and beyond; Chapter 3, for example, mostly operates at a narrow scope, while Chapter 5, at the other extreme, considers pattern linkages across groups of texts.

Chapter 2 is about word-lists. Through transformation of a text into a word-list, and selection of the words which go into it, further questions are raised concerning the nature of the category "word" and "text". The issue of closed-set and open-set lexical items is linked here to word frequency, so we study the nature of high-, medium- and low-frequency items in a word-list. The chapter ends with a study which shows that word-lists are not randomly generated oddities but instead obey underlying laws.

The overall theme of Chapter 3 is concordancing, but first the nature of co-occurrence has to be clarified. Words are like people, their relationships go beyond their neighbourhood and there can be one-way or two-way attraction between them. It is useful to distinguish between mental and textual co-occurrence and so a study is carried out to find out whether word associations match up with textual linkage. Scott also looks at further patterns which can be revealed through resources such as clusters and plots, and ends the chapter with a further study considering the potential linkages of a given word with its sentence-, paragraph- and text-positions.

The next chapter deals with key words (KWs), considering the nature of keyness and how this is dependent on repetition. Identifying keyness, in turn, is dependent on the use of filters and statistical tests, so the characteristics of a reference corpus are discussed too. There follow four studies, which concern first the key words of Romeo and Juliet, then the effect of varying the choice of reference corpus. Next comes the issue of plotting where the key words occur in texts and a distinction between global and local key words dispersion patterns, which leads to a study of how key words are interlinked. The fourth study deals with the kinds of words which tend to be key; a lot of them seem to be nouns but then a lot of words in texts are nouns too, so the aim is to find out whether key words are more likely than other words to be nouns.

Chapter 5 goes beyond the scope of the preceding one to consider the formal patterns of linkage and to analyse these patterns as they obtain between texts, not just within them. There follow two studies, the first of which aims to pinpoint the characteristics of "key key words", to see whether these share some of the qualities of wordlists identified in Chapter 2, and in particular to find out whether key key words reflect aboutness. The study is done first with a general corpus and then with corpora differentiated by domain. The final study looks at associates, defining these and studying the academic and non-academic associates of key key words in the Humanities, in Law and in Technology.

Chapter 6 introduces the reader to a simple corpus analysis methodology (drawing on word-lists and key word lists) which can be used to find out the main lexico-grammatical features of a collections of similar texts. Using micro corpora extracted from the British National Corpus, Tribble shows how pedagogically important features of written and spoken production can be identified. The chapter makes explicit many of the procedures which will be used in those which follow and offers practical guidelines on the preparation and subsequent analysis of text data using simple Excel spreadsheets.

In Chapter 7 a small collection of business correspondence provides the basis for a consideration of how reader writer relationships are constructed in professional settings. An important feature of this chapter is the way in which Tribble shows how one can combine genre analysis with corpus and KW analysis to build comprehensive accounts of language use in specific contexts. While a genre analytic reading of the texts allows the identification of a set of relationships between readers and writers along axes of distance and proximity, as well as the development of a move analysis which accounts for the major structural components of specific categories of correspondence, KW and Plot analysis make it possible to identify the linguistic exponents which are used to realise these relationships.

Chapter 8 draws on a different kind of analysis to investigate contrasts between expert and apprentice performances in academic writing. In this case the focus is on what Scott calls *clusters*, otherwise known as *lexical bundles* in Biber and Conrad (1999). For Biber and Conrad, *lexical bundles* are four word combinations which occur with a threshold frequency per million, although for Scott, *clusters* are any multi-word combination which occurs within frequency thresholds set by the researcher. The interest is that by studying how clusters are used in contrasting text collections, it is possible to isolate the prefabricated units which different categories of writers depend on for building arguments, offering examples, referring and the like. The study in Chapter 8 shows how the performances of advanced apprentice undergraduate writers in literary studies (Polish MA English Philology students) contrast with those of authors of published research articles in the same field.

Chapter 9 demonstrates the use of KW analysis in a diachronic study. Taking a large collection of texts from the Guardian Weekly, Tribble shows how KWs can give insights not only into the "aboutness" of texts, but also into the ways in which news reporters treat issues. In a series of studies, the chapter shows how KW analysis is able to give insights into how contrasting political fortunes of Messrs. Blair, Clinton and Milosevic were reported; how certain topics are consistently linked with the negative prefix *anti* or the more positive prefix *pro*; how gender bias in news reporting can be tracked through the analysis of personal pronouns and titles; and how the key themes for each year of the Guardian Weekly can be identified.

In complete contrast to this large scale study of many thousands of individual texts, Chapter 10 demonstrates how corpus tools can be used in the study of a single, very short, short story. The analysis of a short story by the 20th Century Irish writer Samuel Beckett works at two levels. In the first part of the chapter, Tribble shows how a simple statistical analysis of sentence length combined with a study of the collocations of high frequency items can reveal the structure of a narrative text. In the second part, this time using the concordancer to identify patterning around clause boundaries, Tribble is able to explicate the contradictory and unreliable nature of the text, and the tension between the reader's desire to make sense of things and the ultimate uncertainty of this unreliable narrator.

All of these chapters are linked by what is the recurring theme of this book, that an attention to *texts* is the best starting point for a corpus informed language pedagogy. Rather than seeing corpus data as entirely abstracted from its linguistic and social context, the studies stress the obligation on the researcher to re-connect with the text (and, where possible, with its context of production) in order to build accounts of language in use which will have value for teachers and students of language alike.

PART I

CHAPTER 1

Texts in language study
and language education

It is impossible to study patterned data without some theory, however primitive. The advantage of a robust and popular theory is that it is well tried against previous evidence and offers a quick route to sophisticated observation and insight. The main disadvantage is that, by prioritizing some patterns, it obscures others.   (Sinclair 2004: 10)

Introduction

In this chapter we tackle the problem of where and how one can reasonably expect Corpus Linguistics to make a contribution to language study and how that contribution might match up with the aims and the constraints of those involved in language education. Many of the issues outlined here in this first chapter will be developed in subsequent ones, with examples; here we want to lay down a framework.

The main issues we will focus on concern themselves with possibilities already opened up in a field which promises to open up a great deal more in the future. Corpus Linguistics is still in its infancy. Already a number of important claims have been made for it and controversies have arisen as to what its status is and what its goals are. There must be a temptation for language teachers either to feel that there has been a lot of fuss about nothing much, since learning is evidently a skill for which humans are equipped and computers are not, or else feel apprehensive – how to get *au fait* with the discoveries that one hears corpus-based research has come up with.

Corpus-based methods are just that – methods using corpora of texts, whether written or spoken, that is to say genuine examples of language in use. The established alternative is intuition – methods relying on the speaker's own knowledge of the language and what seems to sound like a possible utterance compared with what jars or seems "un-English". Naturally, these two positions are not mutually exclusive. Nor is the use of corpora new. In the late 19th century, the Oxford English Dictionary was compiled in one of the most impressive research initiatives ever undertaken, using an enormous number of slips collected containing authentic examples of language in use that the team and their collaborators came across. A corpus of tiny fragments, not of complete texts. For centuries before that, corpora of whole texts, high-status ones, were put together and preserved in libraries and then studied. A major aim beyond the preservation of art and knowledge, was to provide models of rhetoric, style, grammar, etc. which could be studied by the young. What has happened in the last fifty years or so is that technology has allowed us much faster and more effective ways of collecting and accessing genuine examples.

Here we take the position that corpus-based methods are merely a set of tools and frameworks. It makes no more sense to claim that Corpus Linguistics is a new branch of knowledge than to claim that keyhole surgery is a new branch of medicine. The aim of medicine is presumably to understand and alleviate or cure illness; with the advent of new techniques and instruments such as lasers, medicine takes on new methods but the fundamental aims remain the same. Some of those involved in medicine may wish to specialise in keyhole surgery, but there are good doctors who do not.

But the matter isn't quite as simple as that. The new hardware and software used in corpus-based methods are opening up exciting possibilities which could not have been envisaged without them. In so doing the very foundations of Linguistics have been shaken; in some cases the movement of the tectonic plates has thrust up new Himalayas where before there was apparently level ground. For example, Sinclair's (1991) corpus-based questioning of the parts-of-speech which were so traditionally established, or Francis, Hunston and Manning's (1996) pattern grammar arguing that grammar is much more local than it had seemed, which meant that by the late 20th century lexis came to occupy the centre of language study previously dominated by syntax and grammar.

The difference between a new technique, like keyhole surgery (however exciting to the layperson and vitally useful to the patient it may be), on the one hand, and a development like corpus-based methods in language study on the other hand, is that the latter provokes a qualitative shift in how the very subject-matter is understood. In medicine, we might perhaps go back to the discovery of the double-helix structure of DNA (just about the time electronic corpus-based methods were starting up) or, better still, earlier in time to the 19th century change in understanding, whereby for the first time there was awareness in the medical community of a connection between water supplies and public health. These are developments which shook medicine up. No doctor after Pasteur could reasonably ignore the germ theory of medicine; no doctor after Crick and Watson could dismiss genetics.

If, then, as said above, "corpus-based methods are merely a set of tools and frameworks", the *merely* is deceptive. It emphasises the fact that one can carry out language study without resorting to corpora and still make interesting and worth-while discoveries. But it ignores the fact that corpus-based tools have a potential to shake the foundations of the field.

Why have corpus-based methods caused an upheaval?

In our view, the reasons essentially have to do with the newfound ability to process large amounts of data and perceive patterns in them. In the history of medicine it may be that the causes of qualitative shift were sometimes that the figure in question was intrinsically cleverer or luckier than others, and certainly this is a popularly-promoted supposition. In corpus-based language study, however, there are two main and quite different causes.

First, we have to thank the technological developments brought to us by hardware and software developers. Hardware engineers and their commercial allies have put on our desktops computational facilities far more powerful than those available even to the superpowers in the 1960s. And on the software side, those who do not develop software themselves may not realise that behind the tools and applications they use lie a most impressive array of tools for software development itself (compilers, debuggers, integrated environments etc.) and a lot of people working on standards and protocols for text interchange and transmission. The results of these efforts are such that modern corpus software, whose applications we shall be discussing in detail in this volume, is capable of ploughing through vast quantities of text in a relatively short time, possibly accessing it remotely, and reducing it to a set of potential patterns.

The second aspect is summarised in that phrase "potential patterns". How so? The process operates in two stages. First, all the effort of a concordancer or a word-listing application goes into reducing a vast and complex object to a much *simpler* shape. That is, a set of 100 million words on a confusing wealth of topics in a variety of styles and produced by innumerable people for a lot of different reasons gets reduced to a mere list in alphabetical order. A rich chaos of language is reduced, it is "boiled down" to a simpler set. In the vapours that have steamed off are all the facts about who wrote the texts and what they meant. We have therefore lost a great deal in that process, and if it damaged the original texts we would never dare do it.

The advantage comes in the second stage where one examines the boiled-down extract, the list of words, the concordance. It is here that something not far different from the sometimes-scorned "intuition" comes in. This is imagination. Insight. Human beings are unable to see shapes, lists, displays, or sets without insight, without seeing in them "patterns". It seems to be a characteristic of the *homo sapiens* mind that it is often unable to see things "as they are" but imposes on them a tendency, a trend, a pattern. From the earliest times, the very stars in the sky have been perceived as belonging in "constellations". This capability can come at a cost, of course: it may be easy to spot a pattern in a cloud or in a constellation and thereby build up a mistaken theory; but the point is that it is this ordinary imaginative capacity, that of seeing a pattern, which is there in all of us and which makes it possible for corpus-based methods to make a relatively large impact on language theory. For with these twin resources, namely the tools to manipulate a lot of data in many different ways and without wasting much time, combined with the power of imagination and pattern-recognition, it becomes possible to chase up patterns that seem to be there and come up with insights affecting linguistic theory itself. The tools we use generate patterns (lists, plots, colour arrangements) and it is when we see these that in some cases the pattern "jumps out" at us. In other cases we may need training to see the patterns but the endeavour is itself largely a search for pattern.

A text focus, a language focus, a culture focus or a brain focus?

We have considered the methods behind corpus-based language research and claimed they have proved powerful in pattern-generation – what about the aims, the focus guiding the work? Here we wish to discuss a set of aspects of language which it is important to distinguish in order to determine and choose a suitable focus and purpose for language study.

For a long time in language research and language education too, the focus was clearly on "the language" itself. Grammarians described the official language, teachers taught it in schools. The aim was to find out the basic patterns of the language, such as that sentences typically have a subject and a predicate. Those who made dictionaries (we shall come to them in more detail in the next chapter) aimed to fix the lexical component of "the language" so that there was a reference which one might consult if in doubt. Self-evidently, corpus-based language studies may have a focus on "the language".

In Classical times, there was an alternative focus: the text. In the study of rhetoric, the aim was, roughly speaking, to understand what made a text have impact. To this end the speeches of those considered to be successful in the arts and politics were studied. Rhetoric may have been displaced in most countries as a school subject, but Text Linguistics has similar aims – to identify patterns in text and to find out how text structures itself. Not just how sentences are structured but how whole sections of text flow and move (Sinclair & Coulthard 1975; Swales 1990) and indeed what similarities and differences there are between text-types. In corpus-based analysis, studying key words as we shall see in later chapters, belongs firmly in a text focus, since what we mean by a key word is by and large determined by a notion of a text or a set of texts which it is key in.

A third component is the human mind. Those involved in the psychology of language are concerned to study language as a mental capacity. For example, Aitchison (2003) is interested in the mental lexicon and how it works. Word association studies identify possible linkages within the mental lexicon. The language researcher may well be interested in studying aphasia (when the mental apparatus is not working properly) or language-learning (how someone comes to grasp some aspects of language easily and others with difficulty).

Finally, there is the culture where the language is used. This is the realm of the sociolinguist, the analyst of how words reveal commonality and difference between people.

Language educators are in general interested in all of these aspects at the same time. They may be appointed to teach a "language"; in so doing they deal with people who have problems understanding or producing a suitably-structured "text"; they need to be concerned with the whole process of learning, which is our mental aspect.

These aspects can be represented as in Figure 1.

The figure is concerned with four aspects of words which it is important to distinguish in terms of goals. The lexicographer and grammarian are largely concerned with problems within the bottom left box; the text linguist or discourse analyst to work with words in terms of their relationships with each other within the framework of a text; the psycholinguist with the mental lexicon, the sociolinguist, historian and political scientist the bottom right box. None of them can ignore the other boxes, for all four aspects are related, but for a given piece of work there will usually be a dominant focus on one of them. We shall see examples of these various focuses in the following chapters.

Words in Texts	Words in the Brain
sentences paragraphs sections key words etc.	memory e.g. tip-of-the-tongue word associations enjoyment priming

Words in the Language	Words in Culture
lexicography terminology, phraseology, etc. patterns of "standard English"	cultural key words, indicators of class and stance, bias, etc.

Figure 1. Four aspects of language study

The notion of context

A further issue which we must tackle here is that of "context". The term is a familiar one, and seems intuitive until it is examined carefully. If an informant tells us that they understood a certain word "in context" or "from the context", or another asks for "a context" before they try to explain a term, what exactly do they mean? How big is the context they may have in mind? Every textbook about lexis tells us that words are to be studied "in context". As Cruse (1986: 1) puts it right at the start: "It is assumed that the semantic properties of a lexical item are fully reflected in appropriate aspects of the relations it contracts with actual and potential contexts." For Cruse, it is through "contextual normality" that one must study lexis. His first chapter is called "a contextual approach to lexical semantics". He does distinguish between "linguistic" and "extra-linguistic situational contexts" (though he considers only the former in lexical semantics) and he discusses in detail how context may affect meaning. For example in "Arthur poured the butter into a dish" the contextual placing of "poured" and "butter" causes an implicit promotion of "hot" from a merely possible quality of butter to a canonical one (1986: 52–53).

However, the nature of context is not developed further. For our present purposes, it will be necessary to consider the scope of a "context". We may first consider a few words, three or four on either side of the term we are interested in (the "node"). This is the smallest context and often it may be sufficient to enable discussion of meaning, as in a discussion of *bank*, where the immediate neighbours *river* on the left, or *profits* on the right may be enough. This is scope 1 in the figure which follows. It is a level to which we will return in discussing collocation (Chapter 3).

Let us consider a real example, from the *Guardian*, 26 September 1994, page 2.

> *Injured actor 'stable'*
> *EastEnders star Steve McFadden was 'stable' in St. Thomas's Hospital, London, last night after being stabbed in the back, arm and hand under Waterloo Bridge, central London, on Friday.*

Let us consider the node *back*. The immediate context *stabbed in the* in positions L3 to L1 tells us we are dealing with a part of the body, not an adverb or the rear part of a building. The scope of this level of context extends a few words: by this we mean that the node contracts relations with items within that distance. It does not contract the same sort of relations with *on Friday*; I am not sure that *back* contracts any meaning relation with *on Friday*, apart from being in the same sentence (scope 2), though *stabbed* clearly does.

Contextual Scope
SCOPE 1: a few words to left and right
SCOPE 2: the whole sentence
SCOPE 3: the paragraph
SCOPE 4: the story so far (up to *back*)
SCOPE 5: the section or chapter
SCOPE 6: the whole text
SCOPE 7: the colony of texts to which this one belongs
SCOPE 8: other related texts
SCOPE 9: the context of culture
EXTRA-LINGUISTIC SCOPE: where you are when you meet the text

For this short text, scope 3 of our node *back* is the paragraph and unusually, this is greater than scope 4, the story so far (which is the whole text including the headline up to *back*). Scope 5 seems at first not to apply since there are no distinguished sections, but we should count the heading and the body of the text as separate sections – the Guardian certainly would. Scope 6 is the whole text presented above. Scope 7 is the other texts on the same page (a murder, a footballer selling off his medals) which were deemed by the Guardian to be related enough to be placed on page 2 with this one – the one above it is also concerned with crime and the one below with a celebrity. Scope 8 (other related texts) is concerned with texts pointed to explicitly by the text in question. In the present chapter there are academic references of this sort, e.g. to Cruse (1986). In our Guardian text above, there is the reference to an extended text, the soap opera EastEnders. But the best examples are flagged twice by inverted commas around the word *stable*. These point explicitly to a text by some person, presumably a hospital spokesperson, who must have reported on the actor's condition but whose very report is only suggested in the inverted commas.

Scope 9 is the culture which we need to know about; it is where the textual world meets the mental one. This is schema or background knowledge. "Culture" means knowing that elephants are grey and that France is a country. In our present case, understanding that EastEnders is a soap opera, that these have actors and that some of the actors are called stars is within scope 9. The extra-linguistic scope (10) here, for you, is wherever you are sitting in a particular room. Sometimes a learner can infer the meaning of a new word from the fact that it was said in a party, or during a wedding, or when it was hailing; this is part of the context, too.

Note that from scopes 1 to 7 we have been guided by increasing amounts of text. Scope 8 is pointed to sporadically at any point in a text, and scope 9 is implicit more or less all the way through the text.

I do not believe there is much contextual linkage in the case of *back* with say *EastEnders*, or *Friday*, but there clearly is with *injured* in the headline (scope 6). *Star*, on the other hand, is linked much more clearly with *EastEnders*, *actor*, *McFadden*; *Waterloo Bridge* with *London* and *St. Thomas's Hospital*, etc.

As we have seen, context is a creature with differing habitats, sometimes tiny, sometimes swelling large as a cloud. These different context scopes will be important to us in our explorations of lexical relations in the chapters which follow.

In this chapter we have begun to consider the relationship of pattern with theory, much as Sinclair (2004) does in the quotation at the head of the chapter. The reduction of complex data to an underlying pattern requires us to have a good general plan, to decide whether we are studying the language, the nature of text, the way the brain processes these, or how they impinge on and reflect culture – or all of these; to be aware of the contextual scopes within which we operate at different times. Theory derives from pattern; pattern reflects theory. In the following chapters we will consider methods (in Part 1) and examples (Part 2) which rest on the foundations laid here.

## CHAPTER 2

Word-lists

Approaching texts

Homo sapiens are about pattern recognition, he says. Both a gift and a trap.
(William Gibson, 2003, *Pattern Recognition*. London: Penguin, p. 22)

Introduction

This chapter gives an explanation of the nature of word-lists, showing how they have a small number of high frequency items at the head and an enormous tail of hapax legomena (words which occur once only in a corpus), and discusses the implications for text and genre understanding and learning. As we examine the word-list, we shall find that there are still more problems than solutions, that there are traps as well as gifts, because what at first appears simple often hides a mass of complex phenomena.

First, however, let us place word-listing in its context as an activity which one might wish to undertake. Historically, there have been only a few types of basic operation which the general language user has wished to perform on a text: to store it by writing it down comes only with the advent of writing, very much later than the original two operations – creative telling and subsequent remembering. Storage on other media (such as the printed book, web-sites, audio tape, electronic text corpora etc.) comes much later still, some of these only with the 20th Century, but can be seen as essentially part of the same wish to collect and preserve.

There are two principles which can guide those of us who wish to go beyond these original operations of creation, recall and storage, namely trans-formation and selection.

In this chapter we will discuss three major issues. The first will cover the kinds of single wordlists that have been used in earlier studies of words and in current computational analysis of texts. These include Alphabetically ordered and Frequency ordered. Secondly, we will consider alternative kinds of lists, including those which give insights into what Biber et al. (2000) call *lexical bundles* (*clusters* in WordSmith Tools), or those which might give us a clearer understanding of the non-linguistic contexts in which words are used. In the final section we will look in closer detail at the distributional features of the high, mid and lower frequency items which are revealed by the making of wordlists.

Transformation

The very idea of taking a text or collection of texts and re-casting it in another shape is transformational in the sense that it changes the object being considered radically from a text which can be read linearly to some other form which will give rise to important insights, pattern recognitions or teaching implications. Thus the early dictionaries/word-lists, such as those of Richard Mulcaster (1582) end up with a list usually intended for educational purposes. One of Mulcaster's main interests was the fixing of the correct form of spelling. This early transformation-of-text is performed by taking a whole set of texts, remembered or in front of the author, and mentally extracting relevant items for production in the form of a list, often annotated. This simple transformation serves to focus the reader's attention not on the message of the original texts but on the form or other aspects of the individual words in them.

Selection

Selection is performed by selecting certain items of interest as opposed to the whole set of items available. Until such a time when it becomes desirable and possible to collect all the words in a text or set of texts, selection is the only practical possibility even with the earliest attempts at fairly complete dictionaries in English (an early one in English but not the first being Dr. Johnson's), and selection can, as we shall see, also be used deliberately in order to focus attention on certain forms in a wordlist created on the basis of whole texts.

Kinds of word-list

With the advent of electronic corpora and corpus processing tools, it has become much easier to transform a set of texts and produce complete lists. A word-list is essentially a list of word-types. A word list program goes through a text or set of texts and reduces all repeated tokens to types; that is, each instance (*token*) of the word THE is counted but the completed list displays THE only once as a *type*, usually together with its frequency (the number of tokens found).

In the next section we will take a series of extracts from word-lists and consider the features they may display, the theoretical problems they pose, and their implications.

Alphabetically ordered

First, there is the alphabetically ordered list (Table 1).

All word-lists are based on particular versions of a text, which may exist in numerous slightly different versions, and which may or may not have been regularised in certain ways by printers, editors, copy-typists and scribes. This particular word-list (based on Richard Mulcaster's text *The Elementary*, 1582) at first sight pre-supposes that words are simply continuous strings of valid letters or characters in the language in question, here English, separated by spaces, carriage-returns, tabs or punctuation.

But this assumption implies that one knows which the valid characters are for the language in question; in the case of English this will mean A to Z (though we will need to decide whether capital *A* is to be considered equivalent to lower-case *a*) – but what about older forms like eth (ð) or thorn (Þ)? Then there are quotations from foreign languages which may well be included, or accented characters that are routinely used in English (café, fiancée, etc.). What about apostrophes – are these to be considered as "valid characters" like

Table 1. Simple alphabetical word-list extract

WONDERED
WONDERFUL
WONDERFULLY
WONDROUS
WORD
WORDS
WORK
WORKETH
WORKING
WORKMAN
WORKMANSHIP
WORKS

A to Z, in which case *father's* is considered a single word – if not, what is the status of *'s*, is that to be considered a word, or a bound word-element?

Other decisions have to be made about the inclusion of numbers, or prices like "$55.99" or part-numbers like "ECT790" in catalogues. They should presumably count towards a running word count, but may or may not be displayed in a list like that of the table above. Dates may feel more "word-like" than part numbers but even so, names and dates are odd kinds of word, in the sense that "Bill Clinton", "Rhine", "Chicago", "2001" are names for unique entities, whereas "table" and "gratitude" are labels for types of entity. One might question whether a word-list (a list of types) should report on only the entity-types or also the unique entities. (In practice it would be extremely difficult to program a word-listing routine to exclude unique entities.) Then there is the case of a text giving election results, where there are lots of surnames of candidates and numbers of votes cast, and a few often repeated names of political parties. If we do decide to include surnames, numbers or part numbers, do we want to see every one of them in a word-list? The answer is presumably not a fixed choice but one that depends on the text being processed.

Another issue concerns hyphens and whether these are to be considered as separating words or not. The hyphen represents an odd amalgam of two processes in English, first, gradual change over time and second, ease of reading. Thus in early English we find "to morrow", followed by "to-morrow" and nowadays *tomorrow*. Gradually as speakers of the language become more familiar with a two- or three-word item, they seem to lose awareness of the component parts and write them all-run-together. *Nowadays* seems to be another case of this. Ontheotherhand, if one runs too many component morphemes together, they may become DifficultToRead so that devices such as internal word capitalisation may get employed, especially in product names such as WordSmith.

Then one may wonder whether *work* and *working* and *worketh* are really to be considered as different words or not. This issue (lemmatisation, wherein a single lexeme |WORK| is considered to represent *work, working, works*, etc.) is also a thorny one.

Finally one may reasonably question whether each of the words in our word-list is really being used in a recognisably unique way. Is *works* in the text by Mulcaster a variant of *worketh* (3rd person singular of the present tense) or is it a noun referring to written texts, or to work-activities? In the following extract it is certainly a noun but it is unclear whether the "labor" is only written labour, and in the text in question there is no other use of the form *works*.

> "But sure I take the thing too be profitable, but where no likelihood of any profit at all doth appear in sight, and the change itself seemeth, neither necessary as too the better, neither voluntary, as too the readier, which be two principal respects in writing, I allow not the mean, though I mislike not the men, which deserve great thanks for their great good will, though their *works* take no place. For their labor is very profitable too help some redress forward, though themselves hit it not."

The point here is that a seemingly "ordinary" word-list presented as above thus conceals a mass of decision-making, taken partly by the author of the word-listing program and partly by the user, though possibly ignored by or unclear to some users. Those involved in Corpus Linguistics have to be aware of these issues.

Frequency ordered

The next issue concerns the most useful way of arranging this list as displayed (usually vertically but possibly in columns) down a page or screen.

Users may wish to see a list in alphabetical order as in List 1, so as to be able quickly to find items of interest, using their familiarity with this scheme in dictionaries and phone books. Alternatively, they may wish to see the list re-ordered so as to bring out certain characteristics of the whole set of words. One such is the frequency (Table 2).

Here we have an extract from a frequency-ordered list based on the same text. Note that in this case, we also see the word rankings on the left, and their frequencies on the right. It immediately becomes clear that transforming the text into a list ordered in this way throws the function words right up to the top. These are, in our time as well as over 400 years ago, the textual glue which

Table 2. Top of simple frequency word-list

N	Word	Freq.
1	THE	1,842
2	AND	1,067
3	OF	1,054
4	TO	1,045
5	IN	967
6	AS	621
7	BE	580
8	WHICH	551

Table 3. Top of simple frequency word-list, with percentages

N	Word	Freq.	%
1	THE	1,842	**5.34**
2	AND	1,067	3.10
3	OF	1,054	3.06
4	TO	1,045	3.03
5	IN	967	2.81
6	AS	621	1.80
7	BE	580	1.68
8	WHICH	551	1.60

Table 4. Top of BNC word-list

N	Word	Freq.	%
1	THE	6,055,105	**6.09**
2	OF	3,049,564	3.07
3	AND	2,624,341	2.64
4	TO	2,599,505	2.61
5	A	2,181,592	2.19
6	IN	1,946,021	1.96
7	#	1,604,421	1.61
8	THAT	1,052,259	1.06

holds *The Elementary* together as a text; these words do not tell us what it is about but are items Mulcaster was forced to include so as to stick within the grammar of English.

The right hand column is not very informative, though. What exactly does it mean for there to be 1,842 tokens of the word-type *the* in this text?

With an extra right hand column showing percentages we learn now that these 1,842 tokens represent 5.34% of the running words of the text. Let us compare the wordlist for Mulcaster's treatise on language from 1582 with a wordlist for the British National Corpus (World Edition) constructed in the 1990s based on 100 million words of all kinds of text (of which about 10% spoken).

The hash symbol (#) here represents numbers or strings including numbers such as "1995", "£55.00", "ECT790".

The items in the two lists are in closely similar but not identical order and have similar percentages; it would be worth investigating whether the slight differences in the first 8 items are (a) typical of the first 200 or some other top-slice, (b) illustrative of the difference in text-type between a treatise on lan-

Table 5. Right-alphabetically sorted word-list (extract)

30	TRAFFIC	3
31	PACIFIC	1
32	LOGIC	1
33	PUBLIC	5
34	RELIC	1
35	RHETORIC	3
36	MUSIC	10
37	PHYSIC	2
38	ARITHMETIC	1
39	POLITIC	1
40	DEAD	1
41	HEAD	2
42	GODHEAD	1
43	BEHEAD	1
44	LEAD	4
45	PLEAD	1
46	READ	11
47	SPREAD	3
48	INSTEAD	1

guage versus a mixed bag of text types, (c) representative of changes in English between 1582 and the 21st Century, or a mixture of these.

Other possible orderings

It is possible to sort word-lists other than in alphabetical and frequency order (whether ascending or descending). Above is a list sorted in "reverse alphabetical order" where we get a group ending – IC, followed by a group ending – AD, etc. (IC comes above AD because C precedes D).

We have been conditioned since schooling to handle alphabetical order; it is surprisingly hard to process a reverse alphabetically sorted list. The point of the reverse sorting transformation is to be able to select words ending in repeated ways and therefore locate (and count uses of) such things as suffixes.

Other possibilities can be envisaged: sorting by true prefix or suffix (which assumes a morpheme analysis routine), sorting by capitalization, sorting by word-length. It would also be possible to sort words according to the number of meanings each one has (requiring semantic analysis), or according to their number of phonemes or syllables (Sigurd et al. 2004), the amount of time the word has been in the language, etc.

Table 6. Capitalisation-sorted word-list

N	Word	Freq.
55	voluntary	1
56	where	1
57	which	2
58	will	1
59	works	1
60	writing	1
61	But	1
62	For	1
63	I	3

Table 7. Word-length sort (extract)

N	Word	Freq.
1	I	3
2	as	2
3	at	1
4	be	2
5	in	2
6	is	1
7	it	1
8	no	2
9	of	1
10	all	1

Table 6 shows an extract from the Mulcaster quote above, sorted alphabetically but with capital letters at the end of the list.

This format will be most useful where a researcher wants to locate proper nouns or words which begin sentences, e.g. when studying the tendency of writers through the ages to begin sentences with conjunctions as Mulcaster clearly did in 1582.

And Table 7 handles the same text sorted by word-length, where within words of the same length the words are sorted alphabetically.

Word-length sorts would be useful for locating n-letter words in any language, and for investigating languages like Lithuanian or Swedish where words incorporate many more morphemes than English can and where a word may easily reach 50 or more letters in length.

Table 8. 3-word cluster word-list

N	Word	Freq.
1	# # #	271
2	IN ORDER TO	158
3	# # IBID	157
4	AS WELL AS	151
5	# IBID P	135
6	# # THE	129
7	ONE OF THE	119
8	THE FACT THAT	117
9	AT THE SAME	100
10	SEEMS TO BE	100
11	THE SAME TIME	100
12	OF THE WORLD	94
13	# IBID #	92
14	OF THE NOVEL	87
15	ON THE OTHER	84
16	THERE IS NO	83
17	IT IS THE	82
18	THE END OF	78
19	UNIVERSITY PRESS #	77
20	UNCLE TOM'S CABIN	74
21	IN THE NOVEL	73

One-word vs. n-word clusters

A word-list needn't be of single words but the mechanism for listing words can be adapted to compute 2-, 3- or some other number of word-clusters.[1] Table 8 shows the most frequent 3-word clusters in a set of essays written in English by Polish EFL students.

Again the hash symbol refers to numbers. The list shows a number of true multi-word units (e.g. *in order to*) as well as simple repeated strings which may have little or no psychological reality for speakers. Here it seems that the multi-word units relate to essays on the novel *Uncle Tom's Cabin*.

It is important here to be clear that calling these combinations "true multi-word units", as distinct from mere repetitions like *179 886 ibid*, does not mean that we have captured anything like the full nature of phraseology. All we get with this procedure is a set of repeated strings. Most of those in the table above show patterns of grammatical linkage with a noun such as *novel, fact, time, world*. Some will be relatively fixed phrases like *in order to* though even this one can be found interrupted (e.g. a Google search on "in order always to" comes

Figure 1. Gravestone inscription

up with hundreds of hits), but many other multi-word units will not be found using this clusters procedure. Linkage patterns in multi-word units involving multiple open-set items, such as *old church tower* or *aimed at the head*, are much less likely to be spotted even when present in the corpus because of inflexion (*aim/aims/aimed*) and interruptibility (*old dilapidated church tower*).

Adding contextual information to wordlists

Consider the text from a cemetery somewhere in England (Figure 1).

I got interested in the text for linguistic reasons, the interest lying in the choice of *but* in *Sadly missed but not forgotten*.[2] It is hardly likely that one would wish to make a word-list based on a text from a gravestone, but it will illustrate a few useful points.

First, the text is slightly incomplete. There is a black rectangle covering up the deceased's surname; in the case of corpus analysis not all of each text may be supplied for ethical reasons or considerations of confidentiality in the case of commercially sensitive text. The text as displayed here is also incomplete, since only a corner of the illustration on the gravestone is visible and the rest of the stone is not in view. The letters R.I.P. are at the foot of this particular stone.

Second, precisely what counts as the "text"? Is it the words visible in the picture, or the words plus illustration, or the whole stone, or the stone in place, complete with grave, flowers, etc. – or is the graveyard also part of the text, in the sense that understanding the text depends on this aspect of the context of situation?

Third, one might consider whether working on the text depends at all on knowing who constructed it and why. In this case the why is obvious, and the who is probably the man's son(s) or daughter(s), but he/she/they are not identified. If I am interested in the text for linguistic reasons, it might be important to know who wrote it and maybe even who engraved it. Is this the language of gravestone engravers or as they term themselves mortuary sculptors, or of the deceased's family? Who, then, "owns" a text?

Other text may be accompanied by mark-up; let us consider to what extent this may help. The following extract of a sermon from the British National Corpus (World Edition) identifies a certain speaker (coded "PS1RE") as a minister called Albert whose first language is British English.

BNC Header Mark-up
<person age="X" educ="X" flang="EN-GBR" id="PS1RE" n="W0001" sex="m"
soc="UU"><age>+</age><name>Albert</name><occupation>
minister</occupation></person>

The sermon begins with identification of the speaker and a sentence number, then the speaker's words with some punctuation supplied in the transcription. Each word is marked with its part of speech (POS) tag, e.g. <w AT0> is used for an indefinite article.

BNC Text Mark-up
<u who=PS1RE><s n="1"><w AT0>*A* <w NN1>*word* <w VVZ>*gets*
<w PRP-AVP>*around* <w AT0>*the* <w NN1>*famine* <w VBZ>*is*
<w AVP>*over* <w CJC>*and* <w PRP-CJS>*after* <w AT0>*the*
<w AJ0>*tragic* <w NN1>*experience* <w PRF>*of* <w VVG>*loosing*
<w DPS>*her* <w NN1>*family*<c PUN>, <w DPS>*her* <w CRD>*three*
<w NN2>*men* <w PRP>*in* <w DPS>*her* <w NN1>*life*<c PUN>,
<w DPS>*her* <w NN1>*husband* <w CJC>*and* <w DPS>*her*
<w NN2>*sons*<c PUN>, <w PNI>*nobody* <w VVZ>*starts* <w TO0>*to*
<w VVI>*consider* <w AT0>*the* <w NN1>*situation*
<w AV0>*again*<c PUN>, <w PNP>*she*<w VBZ>*'s* <w AJ0>*alone*
<w AV0>*now* <w PRP>*in* <w AT0>*a* <w AJ0>*foreign* <c PUN>,
<w AT0>*a* <w AJ0>*strange* <w NN1>*land*<c PUN>, <w AV0>*surely*
<w AT0>*the* <w AJ0>*only* <w AJ0>*sensible* <w NN1>*thing* <w PRP>*for*
<w PNP>*her* <w TO0>*to* <w VDI>*do* <w VM0>*would* <w VBI>*be*
<w TO0>*to* <w VVI>*return* <w PRP>*to* <w DPS>*her* <w DT0>*own*
<w NN0>*people* <w PRP>*in* <w NP0>*Bethlehem*<c PUN>,
<w PNP>*they* <w VVB>*say* <w NN1>*news* <w VVZ>*comes*
<w AVP-PRP>*through* <w CJT>*that* <w PNP>*they*<w VHB>*'ve*
<w VBN>*been* <w AT0>*a* <w NN1>*succession* <w PRF>*of*
<w AJ0>*good* <w NN1>*harvest*<c PUN>, ... etc.

The principles of mark-up are explained in Aston and Burnard (1998), who recognize that the BNC is not exempt from errors (such as the transcription of *losing* in the extract above) and wider transcription issues (such as whether *god* should be capitalized in transcribing a sermon and whether the speaker actually said "*news comes through that **they've** or **there've** been a succession of good harvests*"). It is worth noting that no system of mark-up is ever likely to be satisfactory for all users of a corpus (just as no decision about what constitutes a word can be regarded as definitive, as discussed above) because it is never going to be possible to identify all features of the speaker or writer, their location at the time, their reasons for writing or speaking, and exactly what and how they wrote or said, etc. Imagine the difficulty of determining authorship accurately e.g. in the case of this book where there is a joint responsibility for the chapters, or in studying the text from a chatroom or a blog. And the kind of linguistic entity to be marked up is also a matter of choice: POS, discourse features, text segments, etc.[3]

The questions which interest us here however, are (a) whether the "text" is considered to be only the speaker's words, or the words+mark-up, and (b) how such mark-up should be treated in making a word-list. The most straightforward policy is simply to ignore all mark-up. An alternative would be to include tags in a word-list (Table 9).

The table shows a fragment of the Alphabetical view of the BNC (written texts) in WordSmith where information about the frequencies of the various verb-types is visible. A few lines where the BNC tagging is itself uncertain have been edited out. In the Word column we have inserted in brackets an explanation from Aston and Burnard (1998:232–233). The table shows that forms of BE (about 2.5 million in all) are much more frequent than of HAVE (1.1 million), likewise HAVE more than DO (370,000); other verbs outnumber these three sometimes-auxiliaries-sometimes-lexical-verbs (around 8.3 million in this corpus). Figures for the base form (infinitive or imperative) of the main lexical verbs are surprisingly high (3 million versus 5.3 million others).

To summarise this section, what we have seen is that there are many different ways of thinking about words and texts, no one of which could ever be definitive; likewise there are a number of different possible display formats – the one which one needs will depend on one's research purpose, e.g. to locate words of a specific type within a larger set, or to find out patterns and qualities of the whole set of words in the list.

Table 9. Word list fragment showing tag use from BNC

Word	Freq.	%	Texts	%
<w VBB>(BE present)	517,576	0.57	3,119	99.20
<w VBD>(BE past)	1,084,185	1.20	3,075	97.81
<w VBG>(BEING)	77,806	0.09	2,961	94.18
<w VBI>(BE infinitive)	586,222	0.65	3,134	99.68
<w VBN>(BEEN)	238,831	0.26	3,051	97.04
<w VBZ>(BE 3rd person present)	1,027,529	1.14	3,138	99.81
<w VDB>(DO present)	117,723	0.13	2,907	92.46
<w VDD>(DID)	101,122	0.11	2,777	88.33
<w VDG>(DOING)	17,450	0.02	2,369	75.35
<w VDI>(DO infinitive)	54,685	0.06	2,791	88.77
<w VDN>(DONE)	24,697	0.03	2,619	83.30
<w VDZ>(DOES)	51,462	0.06	2,814	89.50
<w VHB>(HAVE present)	257,197	0.28	3,096	98.47
<w VHD>(HAD, 'D)	394,536	0.44	2,958	94.08
<w VHG>(HAVING)	29,640	0.03	2,720	86.51
<w VHI>(HAVE infinitive)	164,682	0.18	3,027	96.28
<w VHN>(HAD past participle)	19,971	0.02	2,534	80.60
<w VHZ>(HAS, 'S)	250,519	0.28	3,093	98.38
<w VM0>(modals)	1,213,891	1.34	3,139	99.84
<w VVB>(lexical verbs finite base form)	906,874	1.00	3,136	99.75
<w VVD>(lexical verbs past)	1,744,186	1.93	3,102	98.66
<w VVG>(lexical verbs -ING)	1,076,577	1.19	3,138	99.81
<w VVI>(lexical verbs infinitive)	2,081,036	2.30	3,142	99.94
<w VVN>(lexical verbs past participle)	1,878,434	2.08	3,140	99.87
<w VVZ>(lexical verbs 3rd person present)	651,992	0.72	3,129	99.52

Characteristics of word-lists

We may now consider some of the qualities of certain sections of a word-list, namely the different nature of high-, medium- and low-frequency items.

The nature of high-frequency items

What is it that characterises the most frequent items in a very large corpus? If one studies, say the top 100 or 200 words, it is immediately clear that these are rather special words (Table 10).

As we have already noted, most of them are closed-set items, a weft of prepositions, determiners, pronouns, conjunctions, whose role is mostly to glue texts together by supplying grammatical information to a lexical warp of

Table 10. The most frequent 100 words (BNC, listed vertically)

THE	WERE	WELL
OF	HER	ONLY
AND	ONE	MY
TO	WE	THAN
A	THERE	COULD
IN	ALL	QUOT
#	BEEN	NOW
THAT	THEIR	OVER
IS	IF	YOUR
IT	HAS	ME
FOR	WILL	MAY
WAS	SO	IT'S
ON	NO	JUST
I	WOULD	**NEW**
WITH	WHAT	**FIRST**
AS	UP	THESE
BE	CAN	ALSO
HE	MORE	ANY
YOU	WHEN	VERY
AT	OUT	**KNOW**
BY	**SAID**	**PEOPLE**
ARE	WHO	**SEE**
THIS	ABOUT	AFTER
HAVE	DO	SUCH
BUT	SOME	SHOULD
NOT	THEM	WHERE
FROM	**TIME**	BECAUSE
HAD	TWO	BACK
HIS	ITS	HOW
THEY	INTO	MOST
OR	THEN	**WAY**
WHICH	HIM	**GET**
AN	OTHER	
SHE	**LIKE**	

nouns, verbs, adjectives and adverbs. In the top 100 there may be some items which can play both roles (e.g. *have*, sometimes a lexical verb but more often an auxiliary) but the first clear lexical item in bold in the list, a verb in this case, is no. 55, *said*. Then *time* and *like, new, first, know, people, see, way, get*. It seems that the top-ranked 100 words are nearly all grammatical with any exceptions being lexical items concerned with humans and what they have recently said, known and seen.

Table 11. Medium frequency items (BNC)

Frequency around 5,000	
2,100	CONNECTION
2,101	DRESS
2,102	LEEDS
2,103	TRADITION
2,104	INSTITUTE
2,105	SHARED
2,106	ITALIAN
2,107	STRESS
2,108	CRIMINAL
2,109	ADVANCE
Frequency around 4,000	
2,577	SETTLED
2,578	LOCATION
2,579	**SHOULDN'T**
2,580	BOB
2,581	LEADS
2,582	FILL
2,583	PERIODS
2,584	TRAINED
2,585	LUCKY
2,586	STARS
Frequency around 3,000	
3,256	PUBLISHING
3,257	VARY
3,258	ABANDONED
3,259	CONSTITUTIONAL
3,260	SARAH
3,261	FEB
3,262	SERVING
3,263	AMOUNTS
3,264	CHANCES
3,265	CONSTANTLY

Medium-frequency items

If we take a sample of medium-frequency words, what sort of items do we find? In the following set, 10 items were each taken from frequency levels of 5,000 or 4,000 or 3,000 times in 100 million words. Here apart from one modal (*shouldn't*), we only find common nouns, verbs, adjectives (Table 11).

The middle of our large frequency list – it has 378,974 items altogether – seems to be characterised by lexical, not grammatical items.

Table 12. Hapax legomena (BNC)

CEREALE	KRACKERS	SITTE'S
CEREALICOLTURA	KRACUN	SITTEST
CEREALOGISTS	KRADER'S	SITTING'S
CEREBAL	KRADS	SITTYTON
CEREBELLUMS	KRAEMERS	SITUATIONIST'S
CEREBLIS	KRAEPLIN'S	SITUE
CEREBRALISM	KRAETZ	SITUÉ
CEREBRALLY	KRAFCHIK	SITUÉS
CEREBRATIONS	KRAFLA	SITULA
CEREBRISM	KRAFTWERKE	SITUM

Hapax legomena

40% of the items in a frequency list (computed allowing apostrophes but not hyphens as within the valid character set) based on the BNC occur with a frequency of one. The first of these, "*A'A*", appears at rank 227,625 out of 378,974 items altogether, which means that 40% of the list are *hapax legomena*: items with a frequency of one. What sort of items are these in the case of a large word-list? Here are thirty items taken from around the 250,000, 300,000 and 350,000 word ranks in the list (Table 12).

What seems to characterise these *hapax legomena*? Some are clearly non-English words, some are alternate versions of accented words without the accents; there are probably typos and mistakes. A good proportion are proper nouns.

The distribution curve and the notion of a "power law"

The Harvard professor of philology George K. Zipf (1902–1950) is best known for formulating what became known as Zipf's Law, which essentially attempts to relate linguistic features such as a word's length, number of meanings, or frequency in a corpus to a mathematical function. Zipf claimed that "the number of different words ... seems to be ever larger as the frequency of occurrence becomes smaller" (in Pustet 2004:8) and that this can be represented by a mathematical formula (Zipf 1965:24; Oakes 1998:54–55; Pustet 2004:8). Zipf and his students (without computers) calculated approximations for several characteristics of words such as word-length, number of meanings, word-age[4] and word frequency, and in a good number of languages. The texts Zipf and his students used were much shorter than the BNC, of course, but even in the

Table 13. Word rank multiplied by frequency (BNC)

10	IT	923,152	9,231,520
20	AT	524,437	10,488,740
30	THEY	376,311	11,289,330
40	ALL	281,972	11,278,880
50	UP	221,761	11,088,050
60	THEM	167,375	10,042,500
200	ALWAYS	44,442	8,888,400
300	SERVICE	31,243	9,372,900
400	ECONOMIC	24,170	9,668,000
500	DEATH	20,244	10,122,000
2,000	PROCEDURES	5,277	10,554,000
3,000	PURE	3,353	10,059,000
4,000	CLEVER	2,269	9,076,000
10,000	OVERWHELMED	617	6,170,000
20,000	TIDYING	204	4,080,000
30,000	SCORPIO	100	3,000,000
100,000	BACKDATE	9	900,000
200,000	MEBSON	2	400,000

1940s he was able to get access to word-lists and concordances. Zipf's Law, as it has become known, claims that there is a constant linkage between word frequency and word rank. What he noticed was that multiplying the rank (in column 1 in Table 13) by the word frequency (column 3) gave a roughly constant number (column 4).

Plotting such data with logarithmic scales used on both the x and y axes, Zipf noticed that a good approximation could be found to a straight line. The following plot in Figure 2 (Zipf 1965:25) shows Zipf's results computed on James Joyce's Ulysses (260,430 tokens) and some 43,989 words of newspaper data, together with the straight line which Zipf claimed underlies this relationship.

The following chart (Figure 3) shows the same phenomenon, but this time with the aid of a computer using all the 378,974 items from the BNC World list.

The x axis (rank) goes from 1 at the left to 378,974. The vertical axis (frequency) ranges from 1 at the bottom to just over 6 million, the frequency of the top item (*the*). Both scales are logarithmic.[5] It is clear from this plot, with nearly 400 thousand items represented, that there is an underlying pattern. The plot approximates to a straight line but is slightly bowed above the line.

What does it mean? A word-list (and this appears to be true of any word-list based on at least a few hundreds of words) contains a very small number of very highly used items, and a long declining tail of items which occur infrequently,

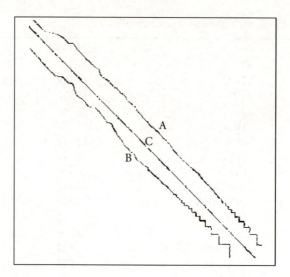

Figure 2. The rank-frequency distribution of words. (A) The James Joyce data; (B) the Eldridge data; (C) ideal curve with slope of negative unity (original caption)

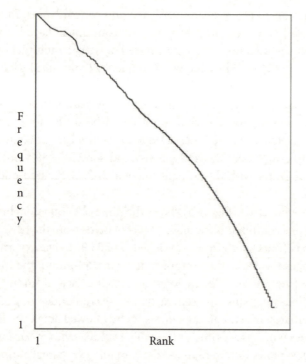

Figure 3. Zipf plot of word frequencies & ranks from the whole BNC

with roughly half occurring once only as hapax legomena. The distribution obeys some regular tendency but is not at all like other distributions with which we are familiar (e.g. the bell curve representing average shoe sizes or IQs). Zipf (1965:21–22) claims the scale represents two principles: one is an economy of effort, whereby speakers resort extremely often to well-known high-frequency items (a "Force of Unification"); the other is the need for distinct words (a "Force of Diversification").

Subsequently it has been shown (Barábasi 2002; and Buchanan 2002 provide accessible accounts) that a number of other phenomena in nature follow similar patterns, including the connections within the Internet (Faloutsos et al. 1999). The distribution obeys a "power law".

The notion of "consistency"

A further notion relevant to word-lists is that dubbed "consistency" in Word-Smith.[6] Essentially this concerns the tendency some words have of being very consistently used in lots of texts, while others are much more restricted to certain text-types only. For example, *your* in the BNC is found in about 80% of all texts, and so is *further*. Yet *your* is much more frequent than *further*. *Taking* (which occurs over 22 thousand times overall) is not very different in overall frequency from *American*, (17 thousand) but *taking* occurs in 80% of all the BNC texts whereas *American* in only half of them (Table 14).

As before, the N column gives the rank, here in a word-list sorted by consistency; the Freq. column tells us the overall frequency, Texts is the number of BNC texts (out of 4,053) and the rightmost column shows the consistency as a percentage. Similarly, words which occur in 10% of all texts vary considerably in their overall frequency.

The point of this analysis is two-fold. First, in a general corpus like the BNC, to distinguish between word-types in terms of how consistently they get used in a mass of texts in the language. Second, if the scope of the research is the genre, to be able to locate lexical items which characterise certain genres or sub-genres. Third, to be able to study text variants (e.g. alternative translations or editions). For example, one might wish to study lexical overlap and difference in five versions of the same fairy-tale, Red Riding Hood, perhaps in order to locate alternative lexical representations of one physical entity such as the grandmother. Table 15 shows part of a detailed consistency analysis sorted by the frequencies in one of the versions (red5). It is clear that the item *grand-*

Table 14. Consistency of selected BNC items

N	Word	Freq.	Texts	%
205	AGAINST	55,336	3,257	80.36
206	LIFE	57,214	3,254	80.29
207	LATER	38,461	3,253	80.26
208	THOUGH	44,056	3,247	80.11
209	YOUR	134,458	3,246	80.09
210	FURTHER	35,825	3,242	79.99
211	WORKING	31,138	3,240	79.94
212	DURING	43,538	3,239	79.92
213	TAKING	22,119	3,237	79.87
214	CHANGE	31,757	3,233	79.77
943	PRESENTED	7,953	2,030	50.09
944	EQUALLY	6,480	2,029	50.06
945	SPEAKING	6,400	2,029	50.06
946	AMERICAN	17,098	2,027	50.01
947	IMPORTANCE	9,628	2,027	50.01
948	FINISHED	8,405	2,026	49.99
949	FORMS	11,575	2,026	49.99
950	ABILITY	9,111	2,024	49.94
951	FAIRLY	6,585	2,024	49.94
952	BRITAIN	19,956	2,023	49.91
7,516	PC	2,583	406	10.02
7,517	SHELTERED	777	406	10.02
7,518	TANGIBLE	594	406	10.02
7,519	TESTIMONY	731	406	10.02
7,520	UNREALISTIC	577	406	10.02
7,521	ALUMINIUM	1,071	405	9.99
7,522	BENDING	732	405	9.99
7,523	CHARITABLE	695	405	9.99
7,524	CREPT	715	405	9.99
7,525	ESTABLISHMENTS	833	405	9.99

mother is not used in one of these versions (red1) and *great* ("what great eyes you have!") is only used in two of them.

What then do word-lists offer?

We saw at the outset in this chapter that using and making word-lists entails a number of decisions about what is to count as a word. There can be no defini-

Table 15. Detailed consistency, 5 versions of Red Riding Hood

N	Word	Total	Texts	red5	red1	red2	red3	red4
1	THE	286	5	126	42	44	62	12
2	AND	151	5	68	10	26	43	4
3	SHE	96	5	52	5	14	20	5
4	HER	100	5	38	8	22	26	6
5	A	83	5	35	12	12	15	9
6	TO	102	5	35	14	22	26	5
7	OF	66	5	32	14	8	8	4
8	RED	66	5	31	1	13	20	1
9	WAS	56	5	31	3	9	9	4
10	GREAT	30	2	29	0	1	0	0
11	HOOD	44	5	28	1	13	1	1
12	RIDING	42	5	27	1	12	1	1
13	IN	47	5	22	5	7	10	3
14	GRANDMOTHER	53	4	19	0	12	17	5
15	YOU	70	5	18	14	15	22	1
16	FOREST	18	3	16	0	1	0	1
17	IT	36	5	16	5	3	9	3

tive answer; it will depend on the researcher's priorities. The more we look at word-lists the more we realise that there is no such thing as a standard one, the shape of the word-list depends on our purposes.

Pattern recognition for the writer William Gibson is a gift and a trap – we cannot perceive the world other than in terms of patterns. A word-list at first sight is a confusing animal, with its high-frequency items rising up like tusks and its hapax legomena lying as flat as fur; its patterns are weird and wonderful. Beneath the surface, though, its DNA reveals numerous regularities which can be useful to language researchers searching for patterns of importance in their own text corpora.

What this chapter has also shown is that word-lists offer an ideal starting point for the understanding of a text in terms of its lexis. Word-lists obey mathematical rules and inherently form into a Zipf line, but re-arranging them in various ways, as we have seen, gives rise to quite different patterns and insights. The different views of word-lists allow us to envisage whole territories to be explored, for example in concordances, the subject of the next chapter.

Notes

1. These are also referred to as N-grams (Banerjee & Pederson 2003 or http://en.wikipedia.org/wiki/N-gram) or lexical bundles (Biber et al. 2000). Interestingly, the term cluster is also used in chemistry, where it has recently been discovered that "clusters of atoms of one element could behave like another" (Ball 2005: 30).

2. Usually *but* signals a contrast; here it seemed to me that *sadly missed* was much more nearly synonymous with than in contrast with *not forgotten*.

3. Cf. the quote from Sinclair at the top of Chapter 1 mirrored in the one from Gibson at the top of this chapter; a mark-up system can easily become a prison. A lot of work may come from POS tagging because POS tagging is readily available when other mark-up systems might be more appropriate for a given research goal.

4. Zipf claimed that the "longer and less frequent words tend to be the younger ones" (in Pustet 2004: 10).

5. Log base 2. The jagged effect at the bottom right in both plots comes from the fact that there are so many low frequency items e.g. the 40% of hapax legomena, whose frequency is identical.

6. The term is also called *range* by Nation (1990) and *commonness* by Savický and Hlaváčová (2002).

## CHAPTER 3

Concordances

The immediate context

> The choice of one word conditions the choice of the next, and of the next again. The item and the environment are ultimately not separable, or certainly not separable by present techniques. (Sinclair 2004: 19)

Introduction

In this chapter we present and discuss the notions of collocation, colligation and semantic prosody. We will show how concordances of an item (often identified as potentially interesting through examining a word list) can provide rich contextual information which illuminates meaning and characteristic use within the text(s) studied. We will also present the "dispersion plot", "patterns", "clusters" and other means of getting at the relationships between word-forms in terms of various statistics. The chapter ends with a study of the relationship between the position of a word in a text, in a paragraph and in a sentence, in which we exercise three of the scopes identified in Chapter 1.

What is meant by co-occurrence?

The aim in general is to identify patterns of unusually high co-occurrence. That is, where two word-forms are found together (co-occur) more often than chance would predict.[1] We shall use the term *node* for the word we are interested in, and *collocates* for those words which co-occur with the node more often than one would expect.

As we saw in Chapter 2, a very large part of any corpus is taken up by word-forms which occur once only (hapax legomena) and these, obviously enough, cannot co-occur with each other in the same corpus. But they can co-occur with the other roughly 50% of the word-forms and will tend to co-occur quite a lot with the words at the top of the frequency list. We can therefore expect most of the hapax legomena to be found in co-occurrence with these high-frequency items such as *the, of, was*; it will then be a matter of determining whether they co-occur more often than you would predict by chance. More frequent items may also, of course, be found to co-occur with each other and here too the aim will be to check for each pair, whether this is unusual or not.

But co-occurrence itself is not as straightforward as the paragraph above suggests; it is useful here to distinguish between two aspects of "occurring with".

First, it is known by any speaker of English that *cow* "goes with" *milk* and *elephant* with *trunk*, in the sense that thinking of one tends to prime one to think of the other. This knowledge (association) comes from the earliest days, before we learn to read; it comes from learning that the milk in the fridge came from a cow through stories, tv programmes and toys, and builds up to form part of our knowledge about the world and about words, our mental lexicon (Aitchison 2003). In this mental world of words, the concept *cow* co-occurs with *milk* much more than it does with chance alternatives such as *trunk* or *gloomy*. This kind of co-occurrence, belonging-together-mentally, belongs in the top right box of Figure 1 in Chapter 1, where we distinguished between 4 different kinds of focus for corpus-based language study, and presumably in the bottom right box too, concerning culture, since the culture generally links cows with milk.

A second, quite different, kind of co-occurrence, deals with the possibility that the word *cow* may or may not co-occur in actual texts (top left box of Figure 1, Chapter 1) with *milk*. This is now a matter of frequency: to what extent is *cow* found in the neighbourhood of *milk*, and vice-versa. If they are found together more than one would expect by chance, then we can conclude that the mental linkage discussed above is matched by textual co-occurrence. And if a pattern like "milk-cow" or "to milk the cow" becomes established in the language (the bottom left box), it will gain the right to be listed in dictionaries and taught in EFL.

A second problem concerned with what is meant by "co-occurrence" lies in defining "co-". The usual understanding of "co-" in Corpus Linguistics has, since the 1960s, concerned a span of 4 words on either side of the node. Sinclair et al. (1969 as reprinted in Krishnamurthy 2004: 49, with original caption) present and discuss (pp. 53–55) the following graph which shows that after about 4 words very little is likely to be added in searching for collocates of a node.

This work was carried out in the 1960s, with the best technology available at that time.[2] Despite this, it is likely that co-occurrence of collocates beyond

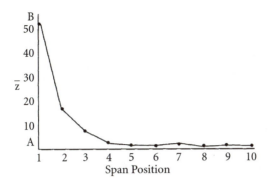

Figure 1. Graph showing average node predictions over span positions 1–10 (original caption)

the span of four or five words from the node will, as the graph suggests, cause useful information to drown in a sea of noise. To make this clear, let us take the example of the word *cow*. Suppose we assume that *milk* can be sometimes found let us say 13 words before *cow* as in

> *I went without a hot drink for those four days. I did get a little warm milk from Rosa (but I am not at all keen on milk) and the warmest place at Low Birk Hatt, in fact, was the cow byre. I think it will be the hay that increases the temperature. I would go straight to bed after finishing my work with all my clothes on, including Uncle's old tweed coat.* (BNC Biography BN6 file)

The problem we have is that it becomes very difficult to show that *milk* is indeed within the neighbourhood of the node, that they co-occur. It may seem obvious with this example and the familiar words *milk* and *cow*, that the two co-occur in our example, and indeed it is certain in general that nodes and their true collocates will be sometimes found say 100 or 200 or even 20,000 words apart in the same text, but the problem Sinclair et al. were addressing is that it is hard to find out which the collocates of a given node are at such distances, when we don't know which they might be. Usually, after all, linguists are not trying to establish that *cow* and *milk* are connected by collocation, but instead attempting to find out the *unknown* collocates for a known node. Sinclair et al managed to show, convincingly, that when you look beyond 3 words away from the node you are interested in, you can get drowned out by the sheer number of words which turn out not to be connected in comparison with the few which are.

An appropriate interpretation, then, of the question of span (or what is meant by *co*-occurrence) is that the span determines what the researcher can in practice *identify* as collocates, not the true typical distance between node and collocate. It is therefore possible in theory for a collocate X to be one which is rarely or never found particularly near the node, nearly always, let us say, some 15 or more words away – we could probably never find out about such a collocation pattern.

In case this seems fanciful and unlikely, consider a useful analogue of collocation, namely the relations between people, about which much more is known. Just as words are found in each others' company, so are people. Is it possible for two people to be commonly found near each other, more so than would happen by chance? Of course – we call this friendship. What about enmity, though, and let us say within a school class? Here it seems perfectly likely for person X and person Y to be commonly found 20 or more positions apart, yet still within the same group. They collocate within the same text but keep away from each other.

There is more. Ought we also to consider the nature of the intervening stretch of text? Does it matter if *cow* and *milk* collocate across a sentence divide, or across a paragraph or even chapter break within the same text? The span we are concerned with might not be a simple matter of word-span, but affected by punctuation or other qualities of text, such as its grammar. In the example above, the name of a cow (*Rosa*) collocates closely with *milk* (in *milk from Rosa*) and the words *cow* and *milk* are within the same sentence, but *cow* is a not a pre-modifier of *milk* but of *byre*.[3]

Meaning, especially, might well matter a lot. For example, in searching for collocational links, one might find a good connection between *open* and *door*, as in "the door was open", "please open the door", etc. But what about

> The Dry Bar 28/30 Oldham Street, Manchester. 061 236 5920 Open Mon–
> Sat 12 noon–11pm, Sun 7pm–11pm. No door charge.
>
> (*Observer*, 23 Jan. 1994, Life section)

The collocation here is *bar – open*, not *door – open*.

Even more problematic than this, is the nature of the co-occurrence, if such is found. Co-occurrence does not of itself tell us much about the relationship between the two items, any more than finding out that person X is usually to be found near person Y does not tell us whether they necessarily like each other. It suggests merely that they belong to the same set – they are often found in the same texts, so to speak. We also have to consider what sorts of dependency relations might obtain between them. Collocation and colligation (which we

Table 1. *Milk* as collocate of *cow*

		Relation	Total	L5	L4	L3	L2	L1	R1	R2	R3	R4	R5
milk	cow	11.2	171	2	7	7	9	4	107	1	7	4	1
milked	cow	13.4		0	0	1	4	0	1	5	0	0	1
milking	cow	11.7		0	0	1	6	1	0	0	1	0	1

Table 2. *Cow* as collocate of *milk*

		Relation	Total	L5	L4	L3	L2	L1	R1	R2	R3	R4	R5
cow	milk	9.1	252	1	3	5	0	3	3	8	5	5	1
cows	milk	10.7		8	8	4	6	24	13	17	7	4	1
cow's	milk	13.8		0	1	2	0	108	1	2	2	2	1

will be getting to presently) both have directionality. That is, the relationship between node and collocate is not usually symmetrical but to some degree one-sided. Just as one person may be desperately in love with another but the other may not return that love with the same intensity, so it is with words.

To illustrate, take some facts about *cow* and *milk* from the BNC World corpus (Tables 1, 2). There are 4,888 instances of *milk* and 1,472 instances of *cow* in that corpus. More than three times as many mentions of *milk* than of *cow* in this corpus, but plenty of each. Using a span of 5 words left and right, we find *milk** near *cow* 171 times out of a possible 1,472 (19%), and *cow** near *milk* 252 times out of a possible 4,888 (9%). Remembering that *milk* itself is more than three times as frequent as *cow*, these numbers suggest that *cow* likes *milk* much more than *milk* likes *cow*.

More precisely, users of English (in the BNC) were more than twice as likely to refer to milk when discussing cows than they were to mention cows if discussing milk. The *Relation* column, here showing Specific Mutual Information scores (Oakes 1998: 171) suggests that the best pairs of either are *cow's – milk* and *milked – cow;* the different forms of each lemma vary considerably in their collocational strength with the node.

How much overlap is there between textual co-occurrence and the mental lexicon?

Overleaf are the 10 commonest word associations in word association tests (Table 3).

It is interesting to compare these word-association results with collocation studies based on the whole BNC. (It might be argued that only the spoken com-

Table 3. Most common word-association responses (from Aitchison 2003)

	butterfly	hungry	butter	red	salt
1	moth	food	bread	white	pepper
2	insect	eat	yellow	blue	sugar
3	wing(s)	thirsty	soft	black	water
4	bird	full	fat	green	taste
5	fly	starved	food	colour	sea
6	yellow	stomach	knife	blood	bitter
7	net	tired	eggs	communist	shaker
8	pretty	dog	cream	yellow	food
9	flower(s)	pain	milk	flag	ocean
10	bug	man	cheese	bright	lake

ponent, 10 million words, should be used for this since word-associations are often prompted orally. Here we are not particularly interested in distinguishing between speech and writing but in seeing which items typically co-occur with the nodes within a span of 5 words to left and right. Ideally, the BNC would comprise 50% speech, but because of the cost of transcription in reality we get 10%.) In this study, the concordancer was set to stop at sentence breaks when computing collocates.

Tables 4–8 show the top 100 collocates[4] of each of the prompt words.

Comparing the two sets (word-association and collocates), we find that *butterfly* has 4 out of a possible 10 matches (*wing(s), bird, yellow* and *flower*) and the top lexical collocate is the third in the word-associations; *moth* and *insect* are not found as collocates but *species, fish, monarch* and *spread* are. *Yellow* may be the top colour in word-associations but *white* and *blue* come more often as collocates in the BNC. It may be that the absence of *bug* is because that form is more widely used in the USA than in the UK.

For *hungry*, we get 3 out of 10 (*eat, tired, food*); the top lexical collocates are *said, cold, feel*. We communicate about our hunger.

For *butter*, we get 6 out of 10 (*bread, cheese, milk, cream, eggs, fat*); the top lexical collocates include *oz.* (*ounces*), *sugar, margarine, melt*. Evidence of butter as an ingredient.

For *red*, we get the highest score of all, 8 out of 10 (all except *communist* and *flag*); the top lexical collocates include *Cross, light, face, hair*.

Finally, in the case of *salt*, there are 6 out of 10 matches (*pepper, water, sugar, sea, taste, lake*), but the top lexical collocates include *ground, freshly, pinch*: again a reflection of cooking in texts.

These results suggest that the view expressed in the figure from Sinclair et al. (1969) above is correct. There is a difference between the same words when considered as part of the mental lexicon and as studied using a collocation span

Table 4. *Butterfly*, top 100 collocates (BNC)

---

butterfly

the, a, and, of, to, in, is, like, as, on, with, was, it, for, from, he, that, I, at, or, has, its, **wings**, her, are, this, by, species, be, but, she, one, which, fish, you, an, not, can, have, his, white, they, had, monarch, spread, **wing**, 100m, 200m, bee, been, f, peacock, so, their, there, will, blue, conservation, knives, large, light, then, when, **bird**, e, if, kiss, madam, out, small, some, stroke, such, these, **yellow**, about, all, called, caterpillar, children, er, **flower**, him, life, man, may, more, most, my, n, old, park, plant, said, two, world, adult, angelfish, back, catch

---

Table 5. *Hungry*, top 100 collocates

---

hungry

the, and, to, was, a, I, you, he, for, of, not, she, are, I'm, in, that, were, be, it, they, but, very, as, is, so, when, we, her, had, if, all, or, said, his, on, with, at, go, by, **eat**, have, no, always, cold, because, **tired**, feel, **food**, from, people, who, now, there, would, like, will, an, feeling, more, me, too, get, their, up, well, one, really, still, then, you're, feed, felt, just, which, been, this, must, wasn't, children, never, am, enough, going, them, out, those, went, after, don't, how, only, time, again, could, do, my, what, even, make, men

---

Table 6. *Butter*, top 100 collocates

---

butter

and, the, of, a, in, **bread**, with, to, or, it, for, on, 1, is, oz, I, you, sugar, 2, as, margarine, melt, that, was, **cheese**, **milk**, **cream**, he, add, but, are, like, until, **eggs**, melted, then, from, 2oz, peanut, 50g, pan, into, flour, some, all, have, heat, frac12, her, over, 1oz, 25g, not, oil, one, they, 4, jam, 3, be, sauce, together, no, she, tea, your, had, his, were, at, **fat**, so, spread, unsalted, we, onion, 75g, fresh, garlic, toast, 3oz, little, salt, their, well, which, 4oz, an, by, cocoa, large, my, pepper, stir, up, put, small, tbsp, them

---

Table 7. *Red*, top 100 collocates

---

red

the, and, a, of, in, to, with, was, on, is, he, it, **white**, as, that, his, for, or, her, from, at, I, **blue**, by, had, **green**, are, were, one, **black**, Cross, but, she, which, you, light, be, have, an, **yellow**, face, like, hair, they, **bright**, out, this, all, into, up, **blood**, not, its, hot, there, wine, dark, eyes, their, brick, has, infra, **colour**, little, when, two, army, over, then, been, my, some, no, old, quot, so, down, if, we, t, s, n, now, can, see, tape, gold, only, sea, through, very, got, who, it's, small, back, pound, 1, house, rose

---

Table 8. *Salt*, top 100 collocates

---

salt

the, and, of, a, in, to, with, **pepper**, is, **water**, for, it, on, or, as, that, from, was, I, 1, he, you, be, are, by, into, ground, **sugar**, at, which, his, freshly, pinch, black, **sea**, have, not, this, add, **taste**, they, her, 2, but, **lake**, tsp, then, them, all, would, worth, if, solution, season, were, an, their, flour, like, put, city, no, oil, had, there, up, vinegar, much, its, little, sodium, when, one, some, more, so, will, has, over, any, been, can, marsh, t, used, well, low, common, fish, we, cooking, only, out, two, s, too, very, about, she

---

within a large set of texts. The match is approximately fifty-fifty. For a better estimate we would need many more word-association results as well as greater confidence than I have in the power of the span of 5 words on either side of the node to capture co-occurrence.

To conclude this section, we find that co-occurrence, which at first seems simple, ends up hiding considerable complexity which corpus methods still have a lot of exploring and investigation to clarify.

Handling a concordance

Too small and it doesn't show anything representative. Too big and it's hard to see the wood for the trees. To make sense of a huge number of concordance lines one needs some sort of guidance – yet the PC is not renowned for its helpfulness. The best strategy in this case is to use some of the resources the computer can supply, chiefly involving filtering and sorting in various ways.

Patterns

The Patterns function in a concordance in WordSmith allows one to see the items which are most frequently found to left and right of a search-word. In the case of the node *cow*, we get something like in Table 9.

At each position the column of words is ordered by frequency; that is, the top item (*the* in most cases here) is the one most commonly found in that position. In the case of position L1, the most frequent items are *a, the, old, of, mad*. There is nothing to prevent a word appearing in various columns, so we can see *milk* in columns L4, L2 and R1, where it is the top item. The adjectives in column L1 – *old, mad, stupid, silly, cash* – allocate low prestige to most cows in the texts of the BNC. The R1 column suggests that *cow* is very often a classifier pre-modifier of a head noun such as *milk, dung, parsley, disease*. This observation

Table 9. Patterns of cow in BNC

L4	L3	L2	L1	Centre	R1	R2	R3	R4
THE	A	THE	A	COW	MILK	THE	THE	THE
A	THE	A	THE		AND	AND	A	AND
OF	TO	OF	OLD		DUNG	A	AND	A
AND	OF	YOU	OF		PARSLEY	IN	TO	TO
TO	AND	AND	MAD		OR	WAS	IN	OF
WAS	IS	THAT	AND		DISEASE	IS	OF	IN
IT	IT	FOR	TO		IN	TO	IS	WITH
AS	AS	TO	STUPID		WAS	I	OR	FOR
IS	YOU	IN	ONE		THE	FOR	SHE	WAS
IN	IN	OR	SUCKLER		SHE	IT	IT	HER
WITH	ON	FROM	SILLY		SHED	SHE	WAS	YOU
HE	WAS	AS	LITTLE		A	ALLERGY	HAD	IT
SHE	THAT	LIKE	CASH		WITH	WITH	HAVE	AS
BE	LIKE	WITH	DAIRY		THAT	OR	AS	I
HER	AN	AN	SACRED		HE	ON	WITH	THAT
THAT	FROM	IS	THAT		OF	THAT	BE	MOON
AN	WITH	MILK	OR		IT	AS	ARE	BE
YOU	I	OLD	WITH		IS	OVER	I	FROM
MILK	POUND	FIDDLE	YOU		I	BUT	FOR	SHEEP

belongs to *colligation*, the grammatical aspect of linkage. We can see classifier pre-modification patterns and other linkages more clearly when choosing the Clusters function.

Clusters[5]

These are repeated groups, similar to the clusters discussed in the last chapter, but here found within the set of concordance lines, using the collocation horizons established by the user (default L5 to R5). There is of course no guarantee that these are what a native speaker would recognise as true multi-word units (MWUs), for they are simply the repeated strings found most often. All the same, many of the items in the set below will be recognisable as multi-word units which hang together in semi-fixed phrases, such as item 3, *mad cow disease*, which comes with a frequency of 19 occurrences in the BNC (Table 10).

Examining the clusters it becomes much clearer that *cow* plays a variety of roles. Some are prepositional phrases which without further context do not tell us much (items 1, 13, 14). Where it is part of an MWU, *cow* may be a supplier of milk, at other times a farming and health problem, at others part of a rhyme, and sometimes (e.g. item 11) the cow is human.

Table 10. 3–5 word clusters involving cow (BNC)

N	Cluster	Freq.
1	OF A COW	21
2	A COW AND	19
3	MAD COW DISEASE	19
4	THE OLD COW	17
5	TO COW MILK	16
6	AND COW DUNG	13
7	THE COW AND	13
8	COW MILK ALLERGY	13
9	AS A COW	12
10	A COW OR	11
11	YOU STUPID COW	11
12	AND A COW	11
13	IN THE COW	10
14	OF THE COW	10
15	COW IN THE	10
16	A COW IN	10
17	COW PARSLEY AND	9
18	OF COW MILK	9
19	AND THE COW	9
20	JUMPED OVER THE	8
21	LIKE A COW	8
22	FOR A COW	8
23	OF COW PARSLEY	8
24	THE COW JUMPED	8
25	COW AND A	8
26	THE COW SHED	8
27	THE COW JUMPED OVER	8
28	COW JUMPED OVER	8
29	A COW THAT	7
30	AN OLD COW	7
31	SUCKLER COW PREMIUM	7
32	THE OLD DUN	6
33	MUD AND COW	6
34	THE OLD DUN COW	6
35	MUD AND COW DUNG	6
36	OLD DUN COW	6
37	THAT THE COW	6
38	THE FIDDLE THE	6
39	THE FIDDLE THE COW JUMPED	6
40	THE FIDDLE THE COW	6

Is *ago* text-initial? – The dispersion plot

Hoey (2004, 2005) has suggested that some words or phrases may be text-initial or paragraph-initial; he identifies *ago* as a word which "is primed for collocation with *years*, *weeks* and *days*, [...] for paragraph-initial position, when it is sentence initial, [and] for text-initial position when it is sentence-initial" (2005: 177).

Table 11 shows that indeed, in BNC written text, *ago* collocates with time expressions, if the search-word is "*s ago".

Table 11. Times AGO (BNC written)

years ago	8,869
months ago	1,355
weeks ago	1,022
days ago	500
moments ago	177
minutes / mins ago	124
centuries ago	123
hours ago	122
seasons ago	79
decades ago	57
ages ago	56
nights ago	30
generations ago	17
moons ago	12
summers ago	8
aeons ago	7
games ago	6
winters ago	6
Saturdays ago	5
issues ago	4
miles ago	3
seconds ago	3
weekends ago	3
yonks ago	3
eons ago	2
evenings ago	2
lifetimes ago	2
matches ago	2
a "fifty-years-ago"	1
mornings ago	1
budths ago	1
Christmases ago	1
Ryder Cups ago	1
fights ago	1

Table 11. (*continued*)

Fridays ago	1
lines ago	1
lives ago	1
lunches ago	1
pages ago	1
paragraphs ago	1
periods ago	1
Question times ago	1
regenerations ago	1
series ago	1
Thanksgivings ago	1
tries ago	1
volumes ago	1

Much as we saw with word-lists in Chapter 2, there is a skewed distribution with a few extremely frequent items and a long tail of hapax legomena, suggesting that *years ago, months ago, weeks ago, days ago* are "grammaticalised", or in Hoey's (2005) terms have become primed. *Tries ago* and *volumes ago*, by the same token, are built up from the grammaticalised, established forms.

Of these, perhaps the most interesting is the one in bold,

> You did a "fifty-years-ago" about a gas-main explosion in Newark the week before last' [...] "I went to Newark for the story too" said old Eddy Moulton.   (fiction prose G12)

a nominalization which makes it evident that this phenomenon is known outside the community of linguists.

Let us now move on to the question of where the instances of *ago* occur in texts, since Hoey has claimed a tendency for them to be sentence-initial, paragraph-initial and text-initial. A dispersion plot may help here. But first it will be necessary to move away from the BNC, which expressly claims not to contain whole texts but samples (Aston & Burnard 1998:39). Accordingly, a set of 14,969 complete texts from the Guardian, January to March 1999, were used, amounting to just over 6 million words, just under 300,000 sentences and 130,000 paragraphs.

It is important to stress here that the studies reported here concern and relate only to broadsheet journalism, without distinguishing between sports, politics, crime or City news, and that findings cannot at this stage be claimed to represent anything other than the patterns in this sample of roughly fifteen thousand broadsheet articles.

N	File	Words	Hits	r 1,000	Plot
1	0 028.txt	1,701	6	3.53	
2	0 013.txt	1,701	6	3.53	
3	2 001.txt	4,379	5	1.14	
4	017.txt	4,890	5	1.02	
5	1 001.txt	2,326	5	2.15	
6	010.txt	1,287	5	3.89	
7	1 002.txt	1,076	4	3.72	
8	2 009.txt	3,444	4	1.16	
9	0 003.txt	1,099	4	3.64	
10	4 011.txt	662	4	6.04	
11	080.txt	4,137	4	0.97	
12	0 003.txt	809	4	4.94	
13	030.txt	2,380	3	1.26	
14	4 006.txt	1,600	3	1.88	
15	2 008.txt	1,571	3	1.91	
16	6 003.txt	927	3	3.24	
17	0 001.txt	677	3	4.43	
18	0 001.txt	3,746	3	0.80	
19	7 003.txt	796	3	3.77	
20	6 009.txt	4,296	3	0.70	
21	9 009.txt	451	3	6.65	

Figure 2. *Ago* in dispersion plot

The dispersion plot for *s ago* in this sample of texts looks like in Figure 2.

Here the plot area is visible to the right of the statistics. For each text file, the left side of the plot represents the beginning and the right edge the end of the text, all standardised to a uniform size whatever the length of each text. The list is sorted by the number of hits, the greatest being 6 instances of *s ago.

The figure, a small part of the list of 1,817 texts containing *s ago, shows several features. First, the number of hits per 1,000 words is moderate, the mean being 2.25 (standard deviation 2.27). The lowest is 0.2, though one occurrence in a very short text (e.g. 50 or 60 words only) can bring it up to 20. Second, there is some variation. 272 texts have at least 2 occurrences but over 80% of the texts which do have *s ago have only one. Consequently, *ago* in the Guardian texts can hardly come in bursts (Katz 1996) but is rather dispersed.

The following graph (Figure 3) shows overall, where this form appears in the text files. The horizontal axis is divided into 8 segments, where the eighth segment represents the end of each text.

The dots represent the percentage of the occurrences of *s ago in each segment. There is an apparent trend for the number of hits to diminish as the text progresses; however, there are still plenty in the middle and at the end of the text. If we compare that with similar graphs for other items chosen at random (Figure 4), we get some like *already* and *neighbour*, which seem to dislike text-initial position in the same corpus, and others which vary.

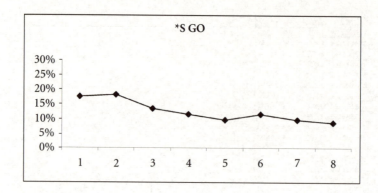

Figure 3. Text positions of *ago* (N = 1,817)

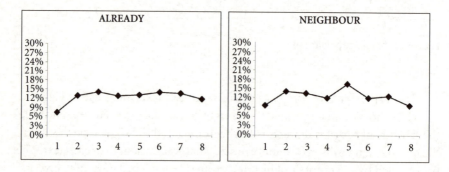

Figure 4. Text positions for *already* (N = 2,503) and *neighbour* (N − 108)

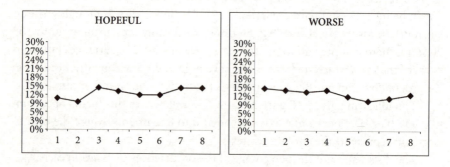

Figure 5. Text positions for *hopeful* (N = 66) and *worse* (N = 543)

The number of texts with *hopeful* and *neighbour* is fairly small, so that each eighth-part segment of the graph represents only some 8 tokens in the case of *hopeful;* one may wonder whether the graph would smooth out to a straight

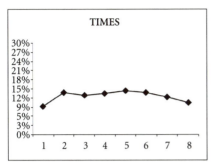
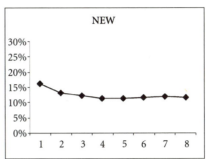

Figure 6. Text positions for *times* (N = 2,015) and *new* (N = 12,944)

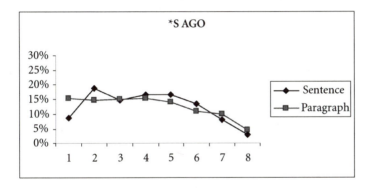

Figure 7. *Ago*'s sentence and paragraph positions (N = 1,817)

line if there were very frequent items. In the following Figure 6 *times* has over two thousand occurrences and *new* nearly thirteen thousand, and the line for neither is really smooth and level, which suggests that Hoey (2005) is correct that lexis has text positional preferences in general.

Let us now consider the sentence-positional and paragraph-positional preferences (Figure 7). *s ago*, as the graph shows, has a noticeably different pattern as the scope of the text unit goes down from text to paragraph to sentence.

It seems to be fairly happy to start a paragraph but unhappy about starting sentences, though it does like to come in the second segment of the sentence (more on this anon). Let us compare this pattern with those from three of the more high frequency items we have selected for comparison.

Already, like *ago*, dislikes sentence-initial position but likes to sit in the second row of the class (Figure 8).

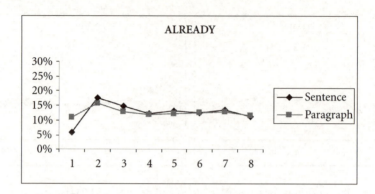

Figure 8. *Already*'s sentence and paragraph positions (N = 2,503)

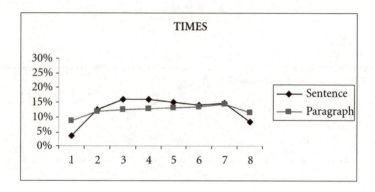

Figure 9. *Times*' sentence and paragraph positions (N = 2,015)

Times really does not like the first part of sentences or paragraphs, and is not happy either at the back of the classroom (Figure 9).

New, on the other hand, likes to sit at the back (Figure 10). Note that *new*'s sentence and paragraph behaviour is not apparently related to its overall text behaviour which we saw in Figure 6. It seems to prefer text-initial position but sentence- and paragraph-final positions.

Finally, let us consider the case of **s ago* in text initial position only. There are 183 entries where it occurs in the first 10% of the text.

What this suggests, when compared with Figure 7, is that *ago* does not behave noticeably differently in terms of sentence- or paragraph- position whether it is in text-initial position or not. It mostly disprefers the beginnings and ends. Compare that with Figure 3 where we see that *ago* in terms of texts is happier at initial position.

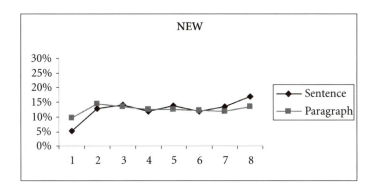

Figure 10. *New*'s sentence and paragraph positions (N = 12,944)

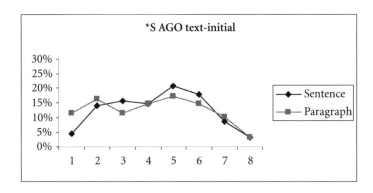

Figure 11. Text-initial *ago* (N = 183)

But Hoey's claim, reported above, is that it is primed "for paragraph-initial position, when it is sentence initial, [and] for text-initial position when it is sentence-initial". The claim is not that *ago* in *general* prefers paragraph- or sentence-initial position. Accordingly, we must now see what happens to it when it is in sentence-initial position. There are 409 cases in the data, where **s ago* occurs in the first 20% of the sentence. It was felt preferable to choose 20% as being "initial", and not 10% as was the case for the text-oriented graph in Figure 11, since sentences are the shortest of our three scopes, here. Even 20% allows for cases like "Two years *ago*" starting a 14-word sentence as well as "As with the performance of his Art Forum band at Ronnie Scott's a couple of years *ago*," starting a much longer one.

Figure 12 shows that where *ago* is sentence initial, it is very often also paragraph-initial. The vertical axis of this figure is higher (limit of 60%, not 30%) than those above because the paragraph-initial tendency is so dramatic.

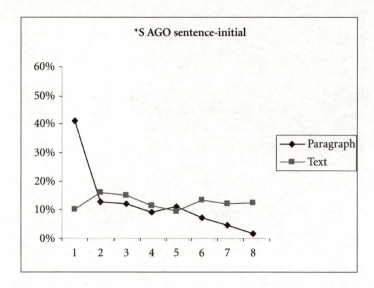

Figure 12. Sentence-initial *ago* (N = 409)

However, the preference of the initial position, so strong in the case of the paragraph scope, does not appear to be matched at the level of the text, at least in these data from the *Guardian*.

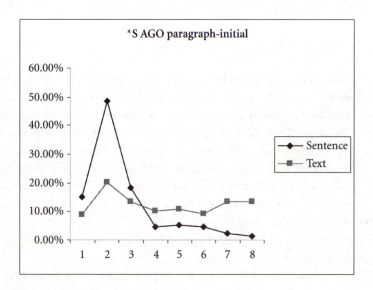

Figure 13. Paragraph-initial *ago* (N = 225)

Finally, let us consider its preferences if we select only the 225 cases where *s ago* comes in the first 10% of the paragraph, which for the present purposes we will call "paragraph-initial". This includes all the cases where it occurs in the first few words of a paragraph, of course, but also a few cases where it comes in the second or third short sentence of a long paragraph (Figure 13).

This paints a different picture. In terms of text-position, when *ago* is paragraph-initial, in these data, it does not prefer to be sitting in the front row but in the second row of the class. It can even be more often found at

	Concordance	Sent. Pos.
41	The race was created 21 years ago when a psychologist, proppin	16%
42	be bottled? <p> Several years ago it would have been incomprehensi	16%
43	om the area. <p> Three days ago, a 400lb bomb which d	16%
44	model. A few thousand years ago, some violent explosive phenomen	16%
45	me computer. <p> SOME years ago an enterprising manufacturer of	16%
46	iographer Lowndes, over a hundred years ago, categorically listed eight	17%
47	70 per cent. <p> Two years ago, the Dutch Prime Minister	17%
48	is true, written almost fifteen years ago, long before the more	17%
49	Gergiev explains: "Three years ago I invited a producer who	18%
50	, Op. 40 <p> Five years ago there was a big programme	18%
51	oak tree. "Eighteen months ago, Mistress Deveril, though	18%
52	collapse. <p> Around 250 years ago the meadows in the northern	18%
53	trends. Compared with 100 years ago marriage is now an almost	18%
54	against her. <p> Several years ago, the university was unsuccessful	18%
55	flight schedules. <p> Two years ago, news of the ozone layer	18%
56	recognised him. A hundred years ago, this man had stamped int	18%
57	yne & Wear. <p> Three weeks ago another prisoner in Durham,	19%
58	address you. <p> Some years ago you kindly offered to take	19%
59	these conditions. <p> Ten years ago, the mixed model	19%
60	here. <p> Almost 70 years ago someone else turned up here	19%
61	did this course erm about ten years ago right	19%
62	en of peace. <p> Ten years ago it was thought that something	19%
63	major advertisers. <p> Some years ago, TVS absorbed Channel TV	19%
64	any other girl would dump you ages ago, you don't know how	19%
65	Duncan Heenan, who four years ago became the first chartered accou	20%
66	not maintenance. <p> Eight years ago we began work in St L	20%
67	originating by chance hundreds of years ago and according to individual choices	20%
68	eminently suited. <p> Eleven years ago I wrote to the then Presi	20%

Figure 14. Concordance of paragraph-initial *ago*

the back of the room than at the very front. Sentence-position is even more dramatic than was the case in Figure 12. *Ago*, in this paragraph-initial position, nearly always comes in the first third of the sentence. By then it has dropped to minimal levels, 5% or less in the graph.

How are we to interpret all this? First, let us recall the limitations expressed above, that these data represent only a sample from a certain genre, not the English language. Second, a caveat is in order about the nature of the data. *Ago*, from the above figure, really does not want to be at the end of the sentence at all. The effect is real, for these data. However, its apparent reluctance to sit at the very beginning of the sentence but in the second row, giving the steep *rise* in the sentence line, contrasting with the steep fall in Figure 12, can be accounted for. It is not at all likely in English for *ago* to be the very first word, and if the sentence is short, even "Years ago .." will place *ago* some 4% or more of the way into the sentence. A third caveat, therefore. It is essential to go back to the data. Figure 14 shows cases of paragraph-initial *ago* (as can be seen from <p> in most lines) where the sentence-position is as high as 20% – because the sentence is short.

The steep rise in Figure 13 is therefore an artefact.

To conclude this section on *ago*, it seems that our data bear out Hoey's (2005) claims but not fully. The relationship between *ago* and sentence-initial position is quite strong, as he claims, and just as strong where the paragraph is concerned. The linkage with the text itself is much less certain. As Figure 3 shows, *ago* is indeed happier near the beginning than the middle or end of a text, but this study has not found any linkage between that (moderate) overall text preference and its sentence-position or paragraph-position.

This chapter has concentrated on the linkages and associations between words in texts, with at the end of it something of a text focus. It is in the next chapter than we address the text focus much more, though, with the analysis of key words.

Notes

1. Or less often, in theory. There are a number of procedures for estimating this statistically, outlined in Oakes (1998). See also Evert and Krenn (2005).

2. The source text is not entirely clear or, it seems, correct, as recognised in a note on p. 47 and some oddities on pp. 54–55 where terms in the formulae used are not clear or appear to contradict the text. A further oddity is that the concluding sentence accompanying the graph suggests that the influence of the node "does extend beyond span position four" (2004: 48) –

I think it is likely that *not* was omitted from that sentence. It seems the graph was computed on the basis of 10 texts, with each one 1,000 words in length.

3. This provides a case of the importance of the distinction raised in Chapter 2 between a unique entity, here Rosa, and an entity type, here the entity cow.

4. Top 100 because of the great number of function words in any set of collocates.

5. Also known as *lexical bundles* (Biber et al. 2000).

## CHAPTER 4

Key words of individual texts

Aboutness and style

> ... strong, difficult and persuasive words in everyday usage ... common in descriptions of wider areas of thought and experience ... they are significant, binding words in certain activities and their interpretation; they are significant, indicative words in certain forms of thought.
>
> (Williams 1983: 14–15)

Introduction

In this chapter we provide a method for identifying key words (KWs) in text. This method identifies items of unusual frequency in comparison with a reference corpus of some suitable kind. We discuss the nature of the reference corpus, illustrating contrasts between key words identified from certain texts using different reference corpora. We go on to show the two main kinds of output in a key words list (aboutness indicators and stylistic indicators) and discuss the grammatical patterns formed. Finally, we demonstrate how a plot of key words in text can illustrate the themes and progression of the text, much as the concordance "dispersion plot" we saw last chapter does, but giving a more complete view of patterns of key word linkage in the text.

Keyness

Many languages use the metaphor "key" to identify people, places, words, ideas as important; the term is used in text databases for retrieval and in practice it does not seem to need to be defined. Keyness is, therefore, a quality which is generally intuitively obvious. Here, though, we must think about the term more carefully; like *context* it is a term whose apparent simplicity masks some complexity. So, for us, keyness is a quality words may have in a given text or set of texts, suggesting that they are important, they reflect what the text is really about, avoiding trivia and insignificant detail. What the text "boils down to" is its keyness, once we have steamed off the verbiage, the adornment, the blah blah blah.

In Chapter 1 we distinguished between Language, Text, Mind and Culture in terms of the focus of language-related study. As such, we see keyness as a mostly Textual quality. Thus, the word 'elephant' may be "key" in a text about the Serengeti, but it does not make sense to claim that it is "key" in the English language. However, it is possible for a given word to be key in a given culture. The Williams quote at the top of this chapter gives a glimpse of how he thought of them. Thus Stubbs (2002) follows Williams (1976) in identifying "cultural keywords" and, unlike Williams, studies them using corpus methods. It remains unclear how one might study keyness as it could apply to the brain, perhaps in the sense that for a given individual certain words or phrases might be "key"; there is a hint at this in the next chapter. At all events no attempt will be made in this chapter to investigate that. Keyness will be textual.

Text Linguistics has already worked on related issues, without I think using or defining the term keyness. For example, Kintsch and van Dijk's (1978) propositional analysis of text identifies text structure, establishing a hierarchy which we might label a hierarchy of keyness. The method starts by splitting a text into its component propositions. For example, the first sentence of the text we examined in Chapter 1

> EastEnders star Steve McFadden was 'stable' in St. Thomas's Hospital, London, last night after being stabbed in the back, arm and hand under Waterloo Bridge, central London, on Friday.

might break down something like this:

Table 1. Propositional analysis

1	S. McF. is a star
2	S. McF. is in EastEnders
3	S. McF. was stable
4	someone said that [3]
5	S. McF. is in hospital
6	The hospital is called St. Thomas's
7	The hospital is in London
8	[3] was so last night

It does not matter much how each proposition is expressed here. We are not dealing with words or clauses, we are handling concepts. It would be possible to replace 1 to 8 with abstract symbols or paraphrases in another language.

Kintsch and van Dijk (1978) then proceed to study which of the propositions get referred to most in the entire set (macropropositions). For the fragment we have analysed, it looks as though [3] is one which gets referred to (technically, becoming an "argument" of a number of other propositions) more than most. Proposition 1, that Steve McFadden is famous, is not echoed in the text, though we should note in passing that it is made prominent by virtue of coming first, an issue we shall return to. The propositions then naturally fall into a hierarchy of prominence, reflecting their keyness. That is, the method identifies the propositions which are most "important" (Kintsch & van Dijk 1978:369) in the sense that they get linked to most of all by others in the text. These propositions, more than the others, are what the text is really 'about'.

A second author to have tackled this issue is Hoey (1991). His method does not take propositions but sentences (as simply identified in the usual way, with a capital letter at the beginning and a full stop). Like Kintsch and van Dijk, Hoey then seeks out the elements which are most linked. A link for Hoey is very much based on the plain text before him, and what counts as a link is a repetition of some kind. It need not be verbatim repetition but may instead look into the conceptual underpinning, as Kintsch and van Dijk do. Grammatical variants (*want – wanted*) synonyms (*desire*, etc.), hyponyms, meronyms and antonyms of a word being considered would count as repetitions making for links, as would instantial linkages such as equivalents (McFadden being referred to as *he, McFadden, star, actor*), inclusion etc. (McCarthy 1990). That is to say, what a given word means in its context is also used as a basis for counting repetition.

There is, however, a further stage in Hoey's method. Links alone do not suffice; what makes a sentence truly prominent is when it is 'bonded' by a pattern of at least 3 links with other sentences in the text. This is essentially because his points of departure (i.e. sentences) are much larger than Kintsch and van Dijk's propositions, which increases the likelihood of linkage. Hoey's method avoids the inherent difficulty and uncertainty of trying to analyse sentences into propositions, but needs this further stage to reduce the pattern of linkages to something stronger, a pattern of sentence-based bonds.

Hoey (1991) and Kintsch and van Dijk (1978) use conceptually similar procedures, relying essentially on identifying where there is conceptual repetition to come up with keyness. Kinstch and van Dijk relate their propositional method to text summaries; Hoey's method actually generates them quite simply: if only the highly bonded sentences are extracted from the text, a reasonable text summary is produced (Hoey 1991). Both of these methods based on patterns of repetition help identify what the text is about.

The method of identifying KWs which this chapter and following ones deal with is also based on repetition. The basic principle is that a word-form which is repeated a lot within the text in question will be more likely to be key in it. A recipe for a cake may well have several mentions of *eggs, sugar, flour, cake*. In our case, it is simple verbatim repetition, allied to a statistical estimate of likelihood. The method uses words, not sentences or propositions, and relies on a simple decision as to what constitutes a "word", namely the presence of space or punctuation at each end of a candidate string, though with minor further complexities discussed in Chapter 2. Repetition here is therefore simple verbatim repetition (so that the algorithm will not see *wanted* and *want* or *wants* as in any way related to each other).

Simple verbatim lexical repetition alone will not do, however, otherwise the word-lists of Chapter 2 would already be good indicators of what is important and what a text is about. As we saw there, the top frequency words (*the, of, was* etc.) have little referential meaning, and it would be very strange to suggest these might be important or good indicators of 'aboutness' (Phillips 1989). The top lexical words in terms of frequency are lexical items concerned with humans and what they have recently said, known and seen (items such as *time, like, new, first, know, people*); these too are not very likely to be good indicators of keyness because they are so indefinite and general. What we are looking for is items like *eggs* and *sugar*, important to the text and indicative of its meaning, what it is about. Accordingly, a second principle is built into the algorithm. Finding KWs requires a "reference corpus word-list" which can indicate how often any given word can be expected to occur in the language or genre in question. This will be used as a filter.

The reference corpus word-list is therefore a simple word-list constructed as in the examples in Chapter 2, with the requirement that it should be an appropriate sample of the language which the text we are studying (the "node-text") is written in. An "appropriate" sample usually means a large one, preferably many thousands of words long and possibly much more.

It is not always possible to get hold of such a sample, of course. Suppose one wishes to identify the KWs of the play *Romeo and Juliet* – what should be used as a reference? There simply are not many millions of words of Elizabethan English available. In the case of Sumerian, there is an electronic text corpus of

350 or more literary texts at the University of Oxford, but no more Sumerian is being spoken or written so the resources are even more small and finite.

A third principle of the algorithm which must be mentioned is a threshold, usually set at 2 or 3 occurrences in the text. For a word to be key, then it (a) must occur at least as frequently as the threshold level, and (b) be outstandingly frequent in terms of a reference corpus.

Once we have a list of the words and their frequencies in our node-text, the program compares that with the reference corpus list of words and frequencies. Now in both, it is likely that the most frequent of all will be *the*, but if that frequency as a percentage of the total number of running words is roughly the same in the two lists, then *the* will not seem outstanding, even if it is frequent. In such cases *the* gets filtered out. After all the different word-types in the node-text have been processed to check whether each occurs at least as frequently as the threshold and more than the same type in the reference corpus, most will have been filtered out but a few outstanding ones remain.

The issue of whether a given contrast (between a type's frequencies in the node-text and in the reference corpus) is or is not 'outstanding' is handled in the usual statistical way. Statistical tests of probability essentially rely on a numerical comparison between a given finding and what can plausibly be expected. Here, the reference corpus, since it is much bigger than the node-text, enables us to estimate what may be expected. The statistical procedure used is Dunning's Log Likelihood function (Dunning 1993; Oakes 1998: 172) or if preferred chi-square.

An example

The following list (Table 2) is of the KWs of Romeo and Juliet identified by the procedure using all the Shakespeare plays (comedies, tragedies and histories) as a reference corpus.

About 20 of the 48 KWs are proper nouns or titles, mostly representing the main characters and possessive variants. *Romeo* is hardly surprising: it is only found in this one of Shakespeare plays. Here it represents 0.51% of the running words of the play. In the text used, character names denoting who delivers each speech were not included in the analysis, so these are all references to Romeo by other characters, plus a few stage directions. *Juliet* is found in other plays too but is here much more preponderant, representing 0.23% of the running words of the text, compared with 0.01% in the whole set. (Note that Juliet is much less mentioned than Romeo: it would be interesting to analyse whether

Table 2. KWs of *Romeo and Juliet* vs. all Shakespeare plays

AH	DEATH	MARRIED	SLAIN
ART	EARLY	MERCUTIO	THEE
BACK	FRIAR	MONTAGUE	THOU
BANISHED	JULIET	MONUMENT	THURSDAY
BENVOLIO	JULIET'S	NIGHT	THY
CAPULET	KINSMAN	NURSE	TORCH
CAPULETS	LADY	O	TYBALT
CAPULET'S	LAWRENCE	PARIS	TYBALT'S
CELL	LIGHT	POISON	VAULT
CHURCHYARD	LIPS	ROMEO	VERONA
COUNTY	LOVE	ROMEO'S	WATCH
DEAD	MANTUA	SHE	WILT

this pattern might be true of other main female characters like Lady Macbeth, Desdemona, etc.)

There are some KWs reflecting important themes which really characterise what the play is about: *love, lips, light, night, banished, death, poison*. However, there are also some items which are surprising in a list supposed to reflect importance and aboutness. For example, exclamations (*O, Ah*), the pronoun *thou* and the verbs *art* and *wilt*, the pronoun *she*.

How can these findings be interpreted? Statistically, these items are clearly outstanding even if they do not reflect importance and aboutness, so they must represent some other factor. All the algorithm can tell us is that these features of this play stand out as being unusually frequent. In theory, there might be any number of causes (e.g. to do with who wrote the play down for publication and when; whether for a Folio or Quarto edition; a request from the actors in 1594 or 1595 for more exclamations, and so on). A cover-term which does not attribute a cause is "style". In our experience such oddities as the prevalence of exclamations and dialogue requiring *thou* need further investigation, most suitably started by concordancing the items in question.

Art is roughly twice as frequent as expected on the basis of the plays as a whole; here it is never the noun, always the 2nd person singular form of *be*, accompanying *thou*. (For more on the role of *thou* in Shakespeare, see Hope 2003: Section 1.3.2b and Crystal & Crystal 2002: 450–451.) It is likely to reflect the intimate nature of the theme. More intriguing are the exclamations. Crystal and Crystal (2002: 158–159) and Blake (2002: 297–298) do discuss exclamations but give little information on these two forms (Blake says these express "emotions of uncertain tenor"); it is therefore worth concordancing to see why they have come up as key.

Exclamations in Romeo

Examining the concordances, the 21 occurrences of *Ah* seem somewhat more likely to be in a negative environment (*Ah, well a'day he's dead, Ah, what an unkind hour*) than *O* (*O blessed blessed night, O sweet Juliet* etc.) though both are also used in mockery.

The key word *O* occurs 157 times in this particular play; in the whole set of Shakespeare's plays it occurs 2,505 times. As a percentage of the running words it is twice as frequent as can be expected from the whole set of plays, which is

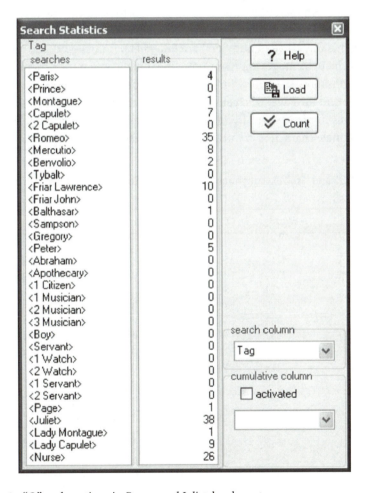

Figure 1. "O" exclamations in *Romeo and Juliet*, by character

why it appeared as a KW. A concordance reveals that there are 9 instances of 'o' as abbreviation of *of*, but this still leaves 148 *O*s as exclamation.

Which characters in the play are most likely to exclaim in this way? Figure 1 (p. 61) presents a breakdown of this.

If the only female characters are assumed to be the last 4 in the figure, at first sight it seems that "O" as an exclamation is equally likely to be said by a female or male (total 74 instances for each).

Table 3 shows both *O* and *Ah* exclamations in Romeo and Juliet, together with the number of words each character speaks in the play, and appropriate percentages.

The *Ah*s are apparently somewhat more likely to be said by male characters (12) than females (9). Taking both *Ah* and *O* together, the chief characters exclaiming this way (shaded numbers) are Juliet (41), Romeo (39) and the Nurse (34). But the percentages are more revealing. First, some minor characters use exclamations more than one would otherwise expect. One might discount Lady Montague and the Page, who get very few words to say anyway, but Peter issues *O* five times in his 248 words, an average of 2%. Second, on average, it seems that the female characters are nearly twice as likely as males to exclaim, in this

Table 3. "O" and "Ah" exclamations in Romeo and Juliet as percentage of character's speech

Character	Words	O	%	Ah	%	O+Ah	%
Male							
Romeo	4713	35	0.74	4	0.08	39	0.83
Friar Lawrence	2774	10	0.36	2	0.07	12	0.43
Mercutio	2112	8	0.38	3	0.14	11	0.52
Capulet	2179	7	0.32	3	0.14	10	0.46
Peter	248	5	2.02	0	0.00	5	2.02
Paris	542	4	0.74	0	0.00	4	0.74
Benvolio	1172	2	0.17	0	0.00	2	0.17
Montague	319	1	0.31	0	0.00	1	0.31
Balthasar	233	1	0.43	0	0.00	1	0.43
Page	35	1	2.86	0	0.00	1	2.86
Total Male:	14327	74	0.52	12	0.08	86	0.60
Female							
Juliet	4343	38	0.87	3	0.07	41	0.94
Nurse	2231	26	1.17	6	0.27	32	1.43
Lady Capulet	874	9	1.03	0	0.00	9	1.03
Lady Montague	19	1	5.26	0	0.00	1	5.26
Total Female:	7467	74	0.99	9	0.12	83	1.11

particular play. Chief of all is the Nurse with one and a half exclamations in every hundred words.

Thus far, we have seen that KWs are mostly connected to what the text is about and are important to it, with some intruders which suggest something about the style and which often repay further analysis.

Different reference corpora

If the same procedure is done using other reference corpora, what do we find? All the results with tests using (a) the tragedies alone, (b) the Complete Works including poetry, (c) the BNC include a core of 26 KWs (Table 4).

Besides those, when comparing with the complete works of Shakespeare we also get *is* and *Peter*, and we do not get *back, lips, thee, thy*. Not much difference; the reason why we do not get *back, lips, thee, thy* is presumably that the sonnets contain a good number of tokens of these types and they therefore fall below the filter threshold.

If the comparison is with the tragedies only, we get *day, Friar* and *Peter* and we lose *ah, art, back, Capulets, Capulet's, churchyard, Juliet's, kinsman, light, lips, married, monument, poison, slain, thee, thy, torch, Tybalt's, vault* and *watch*. This suggests that these word-types are somewhat more likely to be common to the tragedies as opposed to the histories and comedies.

If the comparison is with the whole of the BNC, spoken component included, we get an additional 331 KWs. Many of these are characteristic of the language of the time of Shakespeare (*adieu, alack, anon, ay, bawd* etc.). The first 50 in order of keyness are shown in Table 5 where the 19 items in bold are in common with the core 26 (the remaining 7 occurring further down the list).

A rather different procedure for selecting the reference corpus was used by Culpeper (2002), analysing six main characters of the play (Romeo, Juliet, Friar Lawrence, Nurse, Capulet and Mercutio, chosen as those with the most

Table 4. KWs of *Romeo and Juliet* common to various reference corpora

BANISHED	FRIAR	MONTAGUE	THOU
BENVOLIO	JULIET	NIGHT	THURSDAY
CAPULET	LADY	NURSE	TYBALT
CELL	LAWRENCE	O	VERONA
COUNTY	LOVE	PARIS	WILT
DEAD	MANTUA	ROMEO	
DEATH	MERCUTIO	ROMEO'S	

Table 5. 1st 50 KWs of *Romeo and Juliet* vs. BNC

THOU	I	DEATH	COME
THY	ENTER	EXIT	ERE
THEE	JULIET	ROMEO'S	FAIR
ROMEO	EXEUNT	BENVOLIO	HEAVEN
FRIAR	SHALL	NIGHT	MANTUA
O	TIS	I'LL	MADAM
MY	WILT	MORROW	CAPULET'S
TYBALT	NURSE	DOST	SERVANT
HATH	HAST	ART	SLAIN
CAPULET	MONTAGUE	SIR	ALACK
ME	LADY	DEAD	FAREWELL
LOVE	AY	SWEET	
DOTH	MERCUTIO	NAY	

lines in the play). Instead of comparing these with reference corpora which are much larger than the play in question, as we do here, he compared the set of lines of each character in turn with the combined set of lines of the other 5 main characters. In this way, the 5,000 words spoken by Romeo are compared with approximately 14,000 words by the other five characters. This procedure throws up a rather different set of KWs than those above, much more character-specific.

What the comparisons above seem to show is that while the choice of reference corpus is important, above a certain size, the procedure throws up a robust core of KWs whichever the reference corpus used. These core KWs have largely but not exclusively to do with what the text is about; a few others are usually found which reflect some other stylistic feature. A more focussed reference corpus selection as used by Culpeper (2002) may enable us to avoid much of this common core and home in on individual difference.

The issue of reference corpus selection is far from decided. There are two related questions, the size of the reference corpus and what it should contain. On the question of size, Berber Sardinha (2004: 101–103) suggests that the larger the reference corpus, the more KWs will be detected, which matches the results above, and suggests a formula for predicting this:

Equation 1. Berber's formula for predicting number of KWs

$$\text{KWs} = 95.890582 + 0.11432 \times N + 0.009217 \times R - 0.000105 \times S$$

where
- N = node text tokens,
- R = reference corpus types
- S = reference corpus tokens

(Berber Sardinha 2004: 102, adapted)

He suggests that a reference corpus should be about 5 times the size of the node text. This does not invalidate choosing one much bigger, of course! In terms of the composition of the reference corpus, much further research is needed before we can confidently offer a rule of thumb, if one exists. In any case the research purpose is fundamental: in our experience, even the use of a clearly inappropriate reference corpus as in the case of the BNC for studying a Shakespeare play may well suggest useful items to chase up using the concordancer.

Where do the KWs come in the text?

Another issue of interest, since keyness is a textual matter as discussed above, is where in the text they are found and whether they link up with each other to any extent. The following plot shows the KWs sorted in order of keyness. The left and right edge lines, as with the dispersion plot discussed in Chapter 3, represent the beginning and end of the play and each vertical mark stands for an occurrence of the KW in question.

The plot shows a concentration of *Romeo* in the middle of the play, and the exclamation *O* around the same place but also concentrated towards the tragic final, where we also see increasing references to *death*. *Love* is more in-

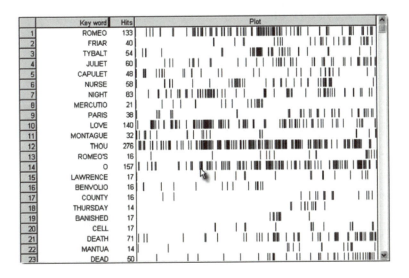

Figure 2. KW plot of *Romeo and Juliet* – global

tensely represented in the first half of the play. There are bursts (Katz 1996) of references to *banished* and *Thursday* in the middle.

Local versus global KWs

In the plot above, the KW *thou* is global – that is, dispersed more or less evenly through the text. A much more localised KW is *banished*, because banishment only begins to be an issue in Act III Scene 2.

Consider another example, this time taken from BNC text A8H. It clearly deals with investments. The plot, here sorted so as to bring the local KWs to the top, shows that a number of business issues, people and companies are dealt with quite locally.

Links between KWs

We have just seen that KWs can be globally spread or locally concentrated in bursts. Another aspect of KWs worth exploring concerns the linkages between KWs as collocational neighbours. KWs, by the above description, are impor- tant to a whole text, but if we narrow our horizons to a more local scope, a few

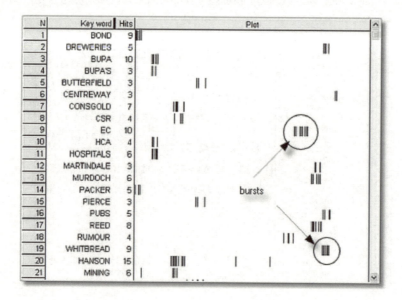

Figure 3. KW plot of BNC text A8H – local

Table 6. KW links (*Romeo and Juliet*)

Key word	Links	Hits	10 Most-Linked Kws
ROMEO	36	128	Benvolio, Juliet, banished, night, Tybalt, art, dead, O, thou, is
TYBALT	23	53	Capulet, dead, kinsman, art, O, Mercutio, slain, is, thou, Romeo
JULIET	30	57	she, O, lady, thou, thee, thy, dead, Romeo, Nurse, is
CAPULET	16	40	thee, Friar, Tybalt, Juliet, Montague, is, Paris, Capulet's, nurse, Lady
NURSE	18	56	thy, she, Peter, thee, is, Juliet, Capulet, thou, Lady, O
NIGHT	19	83	light, torch, O, she, thy, thee, love, Romeo, thou, is
MERCUTIO	13	20	she, O, kinsman, is, thy, thou, lady, Romeo, Tybalt, Benvolio
PARIS	25	36	Thursday, married, Lawrence, Friar, love, is, Romeo, dead, Capulet, County
LOVE	21	140	Paris, Lady, death, night, she, thee, thou, is, O, thy
MONTAGUE	15	26	thee, Benvolio, O, thy, art, Lady, Romeo, thou, Capulet, is
THOU	33	276	death, night, O, love, is, Romeo, thee, wilt, thy, art
FRIAR	20	38	Romeo, Nurse, Capulet, Lady, Mantua, Paris, O, is, cell, Lawrence
ROMEO'S	16	16	she, dead, banished, Romeo, thou, Friar, Tybalt's, watch, O, is
O	37	157	Juliet, Friar, she, Nurse, thee, thy, Romeo, thou, love, is

words either side of our node as discussed in earlier chapters, we find linkages between KWs which not only share textual keyness but local proximity. Table 6 shows KWs in *Romeo and Juliet* ordered by keyness. It also displays the number of collocational links they contract, in this case using a collocational horizon of 5 words to left and right of the node. To the right is a column of hits (the number of instances of the KW type).

Looking at the second row, *Tybalt* is found 53 times in the play, and within the collocational horizons 5 left to 5 right, 23 other KWs were also found as KWs. That is to say there were altogether 23 links (23 different KW types), found near *Tybalt*. Here the 10 most often linked are shown. They are, in order of frequency reading from right to left in the table, *Romeo* (most often of all KWs found within the horizons), then *thou, is, slain, Mercutio, O, art, kinsman, dead* and *Capulet*.

The table has several interesting features. First, the number of hits has little to do with keyness. A word can be key even if it occurs only a few times, such as *Romeo's*. The most frequent word of all in the Shakespeare plays (*and*) is not a KW.

Second, the number of links varies considerably. Linkedness is clearly related to frequency in general, but there is great variation. The KW *vault* occurs 9 times, and has only one linked word (*death*). Naturally, the more instances of each KW are present in the text, the more likely it becomes that other KWs will also be found collocationally linked, or, put the other way, if *vault* occurs only 9 times in the play, it could hardly contract as many links as, say, *love*, which occurs 140 times. The KW exclamation *O*, as we have already noticed, occurs a great number of times, as do *love* and *thou*, yet each contracts only a moderate number of linkages. The item which has the highest number of links in the table is *O*, though in the whole data set from which the table is extracted, the highest KW of all in terms of links is *is*.

KW linkages are not, it seems, like ordinary collocational linkages since they require both node and collocate to be "key". What then naturally brings KWs together? In standard collocation, nodes and collocates like *strong tea* and *cause .. accident* come together in part because speakers wish to classify the tea they drink in standard ways or because they will naturally want to discuss the causes of accidents so as to avoid them in future. In the case of KWs, this natural association, brought about by the (here fictional) state of affairs, will also happen (*love .. death, Romeo .. slain*, etc.: there is a connection in the play between love and death and between Romeo and slaughter). But beyond this, a narrow horizon such as 5 to left and 5 to right will also, it seems, often pick up names such as *Friar Lawrence, Lady Capulet, County Paris*, etc. There are at least 37 proper nouns in the table above, even if we do not count *lady, nurse* or *friar*. This issue, proper nouns, is one to which we return shortly.

Wide- and narrow-span linkages

What would happen if we looked at KW linkages with a greater span, say 20 words? Table 7 shows linkages where the gap between KW-node and KW-collocate is 11 to 25 words either left or right. This means that in many cases we are crossing one or more speech boundaries, operating with a greater scope (Chapter 1) than previously, and excluding linkages between close neighbours which characterise the bursts of KWs we saw in the plot above.

This table shows items where the linkage is much greater than that of most collocation studies (as discussed in Chapter 3 in relation to collocation), since it excludes linkage with immediate neighbours and allows only linkages between items 11 to 25 words apart. Items which are linked KWs in this and the last two tables are in bold. The two columns in the first of these tables showing hits and links are omitted in the second.

A first finding is that there is still considerable overlap. That is, *Romeo* is still linked to *night* whether as a close collocate within 5 words, or as one between 11 and 25 words away. There are only 48 items which are new in the table

Table 7. KW links with span 15–25 words left & right

Key word	10 Most-Linked KWs
ROMEO	death, **night**, **Tybalt**, lady, love, thee, O, thy, **thou**, is
TYBALT	**dead**, Benvolio, death, **art**, thee, thy, O, **Romeo**, is, **thou**
JULIET	**dead**, she, love, **thy**, Romeo, Paris, O, thou, thee, **is**
CAPULET	love, ah, **Friar**, **Tybalt**, Romeo, thy, thou, **Lady**, O, is
NURSE	**Juliet**, Romeo, light, **she**, **Peter**, O, **thou**, **thee**, night, is
NIGHT	O, wilt, Nurse, **she**, **thy**, Romeo, thee, love, **thou**, is
MERCUTIO	O, **thou**, **Tybalt**, is
PARIS	night, Nurse, thou, O, **County**, she, death, Juliet, is
LOVE	Juliet, art, Romeo, **she**, night, O, **thee**, **thy**, **thou**, is
MONTAGUE	dead, **Romeo**, **thee**, love, night, **thou**, is, O
THOU	Tybalt, **death**, **night**, Romeo, **art**, O, love, thee, thy, is
FRIAR	thee, **Capulet**, thy, poison, night, **cell**, Romeo, thou, is, O
ROMEO'S	**thou**, O, is
O	Montague, Lady, **Romeo**, death, **she**, thy, thee, love, thou, is

above and therefore represent wide-span linkages, as opposed to 76 which are repeated, found in both narrow-span and wide-span examinations. The most common linkages (*is, O, thou, thee*) are omnipresent and would be picked up using any system of linkage whatever the span, because such items are sprinkled throughout, as shown in the plot below, sorted by dispersion with the most widespread items at the top of the list.

Second, there are only 23 proper nouns as opposed to the 37 we found in the earlier table. The wider span of Table 6 can no longer pick up contiguous proper noun strings such as *Friar Lawrence*. Such a linkage does not so much represent what the text is about as the multi-word nature of lexemes like *Friar Lawrence, County Paris*, etc. Accordingly we can assume that the other proper noun linkages such as *Romeo:Tybalt* or *Juliet:Romeo* do represent aboutness in the sense that there is a connection between Romeo and Tybalt in the play: Romeo is first taunted by and then kills Tybalt.

	Key word	Hits	Plot
1	IS	342	
2	THEE	139	
3	SHE	109	
4	THOU	276	
5	LADY	62	
6	O	157	
7	JULIET	60	

Figure 4. *Romeo and Juliet* – the most dispersed KWs

We have seen that KWs are linked according to various types of pattern and that a wide span may filter out the MWU KWs represented by proper nouns. It is now time to turn to the general issue of the part of speech of KWs. In particular, is there a tendency for proper nouns to be key?

KWs and part of speech

We have already noted the apparent tendency for proper nouns to appear in key-word lists. This is not because the software in any way singles them out – in fact it doesn't know the difference unless the text is tagged. It can only be because in some sense the use of proper nouns in text has some special characteristic relating to frequency. One still unresearched possibility is that a proper noun may be somewhat less likely to be anaphorised as *he, she, it* or *there*, perhaps because in the world being described there are lots of male and female characters which might cause ambiguity. Alternatively, it might be that proper nouns appear prominent because we are dealing with a play, where characters are especially important to the overall purpose, and where each character relates intensely to the others.

First, however, it is important to establish some baseline facts. Here we investigate the apparent tendency of proper nouns to stand out in comparison with other parts of speech (POS) without yet being able to know why that might be. In order to do this, the whole BNC was re-tagged so that each tag followed the word it related to. The very detailed set of over 60 BNC tags listed in Aston and Burnard (1998: 231–233) was reduced to 20, e.g. reducing all verb forms to _VB and all nouns apart from proper nouns to _N. To exemplify, a fragment like "<w NN1>problem" became "problem_N". It was then possible to treat the underscore character as a valid character and build a word list. As might be expected, the top two forms in frequency were THE_DET and OF_PRP.

1000 BNC texts (spoken and written) were then randomly selected and key word lists created for each. These were then fed into a database and separated according to word class. Table 8 shows the major 20 POS based on the code tables supplied.

The table shows a series of columns, first of all considering the 1000 texts and their KWs. There were 10,691 different nouns which came up as key. Nearly 50% of the KWs were nouns. If instead of considering the KW-types we consider the instances of each one (KW-tokens), we get nearly 2 million, representing just under a quarter (23.38%) of the POS. (The distinction has to

Table 8. KWs and part of speech

Category	Frequency as KW types	% of types	Freq as KW tokens	% of KW tokens	Frequency in word-list as types >= 3	% of types	Freq as tokens	% of tokens
noun	10691	47.94	1780663	23.38	25234	40.03	3894819	19.59
determiner	44	0.20	967025	12.70	59	0.09	2785962	14.01
preposition	98	0.44	854369	11.22	133	0.21	2633877	13.25
pronoun	71	0.32	797694	10.47	87	0.14	1369518	6.89
verb	2707	12.14	474855	6.23	8155	12.94	1776994	8.94
verb BE	25	0.11	472891	6.21	33	0.05	982447	4.94
adjective	3001	13.46	408134	5.36	8725	13.84	1258228	6.33
proper noun	4766	21.37	398730	5.23	18721	29.70	720214	3.62
conjunction	38	0.17	383136	5.03	53	0.08	1327326	6.68
adverb	600	2.69	311646	4.09	1447	2.30	1230458	6.19
possessive s	11	0.05	189461	2.49	12	0.02	343027	1.73
verb HAVE	11	0.05	137627	1.81	17	0.03	312709	1.57
modal	23	0.10	126067	1.66	28	0.04	321011	1.61
infinitive TO	5	0.02	102423	1.34	5	0.01	388089	1.95
interjection	66	0.30	70821	0.93	121	0.19	85878	0.43
cardinal numeral	78	0.35	54133	0.71	120	0.19	191262	0.96
verb DO	10	0.04	35879	0.47	12	0.02	94195	0.47
alphabetical symbol	28	0.13	19526	0.26	39	0.06	33536	0.17
ordinal number	24	0.11	17335	0.23	30	0.05	72026	0.36
existential THERE	5	0.02	14443	0.19	7	0.01	59414	0.30
Total	22302		7616858		63038		19880990	

be made, since determiners represent only 0.2% of the types but over 12% of the tokens. The question we are trying to answer is, "is our initial impression that there are a lot of proper nouns amongst the KWs well founded?", and to answer it we need to consider the likelihood of a given KW instance (token) being a proper noun.)

The rightmost 4 columns give data on the same texts, regardless of key-ness. However, for this purpose, only word-types with a frequency of 3 or more could be used, since KWs by definition have to occur above a certain threshold (by default set at 3 occurrences) before they may be considered key. Accordingly the shaded columns show percentages of the various parts of speech as KW-tokens or as tokens overall in the set of BNC texts. As for the shading in the left column, this represents cases where the POS is higher when key. The data are sorted by the "% as KW tokens" column.

It seems that the items which are most likely in general to be key are nouns, determiners, prepositions, pronouns. These 4 classes account for about 57% of the KW-types. However, the word-classes which are most outstanding as KWs as compared with their regular use in the language, are the shaded items in the left column. If we place these in order by contrasting the percentages in the 5th and last columns, we get the following order (Table 9).

Table 9. Parts of speech most likely to become key

interjection	2.2 times as likely
pronoun	1.5
alphabetical symbol	1.5
proper noun	1.4
possessive -s	1.4
verb BE	1.3
noun	1.2

These results suggest that proper nouns are indeed more likely to be key and that nouns and proper nouns will make up a good part of a KW list, nearly 70% of the KW types. It remains to be investigated in more detail why inter-jections in general should tend to be key. In the case of the O we saw in Romeo and Juliet, there seemed to be a connection with the characters uttering the exclamation, but this may also have been intermingled with gender and other differences such as choice of interjection.

In the next chapter we shall be taking these issues further, looking at KWs in connection with genres and focussing on the nature of KW linkage.

## CHAPTER 5

Key words and genres

The total meaning of a concept is experienced by standing at its control center in a network and looking outward along all of its relational links in that knowledge space. (de Beaugrande 1980:68)

Introduction

This chapter takes the issues in Chapter 4 one level higher, by discussing the analysis of hundreds or thousands of texts in a "key words database". In this account we will explain the notion of "association" (the contextual relationship between words that are key in the same texts) and show how in a database analysis this is revealing of stereotype and powerful linkages between words which are important for language learning because they are commonly associated. We will explore and revise the notion of a "key key word". To do so, it will be useful to go further into notions of KW linkage and what this means.

Keyword linkage between texts

We have been considering keyness as "a quality words may have in a given text or set of texts, suggesting that they are important, they reflect what the text is really about" (Chapter 4) and this means that items which share keyness in the same text have **co-keyness**, which we should now formally define as *shared keyness in the same text*. We must recognize, however, that the extent of "the same text" is not always clear-cut as we saw in the chapter on word lists, since more or less information (images, tags, authorial information) may be included within a text, and as we saw in Chapter 1, there are important connections between texts. Nevertheless, what we saw in the last chapter were KWs of Romeo and Juliet which shared keyness, therefore "had co-keyness" and "were co-key".

We now begin to consider the linkages between the KWs of a text and other words which are not in the same text.

An early example of this, which used human beings to identify KWs, is reported by Andor (1989). He considers key words as identified intuitively by 80 subjects reading the same text by asking them to identify "words or chains of words which you think have dominance over the occurrence of others (items that could function as key-words in the passage)" (1989:31).[1]

Andor then takes 5 of the KWs so identified and asks 30 different subjects to produce word-associations for each. His aim is to investigate to what extent KWs reflect the structure of the text in question by triggering "socio-culturally conditioned knowledge structures" or "frames" in the reader. He finds that the word associations to some extent match up with the tone of the text and argues that the associations which words have prepare the reader to grasp the coherence. The point here, for our purposes, is that Andor too establishes connections between KWs and other words not necessarily mentioned in the text. In his case the linkage runs between text and brain and between text and culture (see Figure 1 in Chapter 1).

In order to study the issue of keyword linkage between a text or a set of texts and other sets of texts more fully it will, however, be necessary to take a detour to consider the formal qualities of KW linkage.

Formal patterns of Keyword linkage

Jones (1971) in her work with KWs for text retrieval, therefore like us here considering both the single text and its linkages with many texts in an extensive database, formalises relationships (Figure 1).

Strings occur where a series of KWs are connected one to the next within a text, but there is no connection between non-adjacent nodes. *Love* is connected to *death* in Romeo & Juliet; *death* might be connected to *jealousy* in Othello, *jealousy* to *madness* in King Lear.

In the case of a star linkage, one central KW is shared in linkage by several texts: *love* by *Romeo & Juliet, Midsummer Night's Dream, As You Like It* and the sonnets, for example. A clique is more connected, since it has a set of multiply inter-connected elements: *love* and *death* and *jealousy* and *madness* might turn out to form a potential clique in the Shakespeare plays, though this would need to be proved. Clumps are also multiply inter-connected like cliques; however, they also have linkages to other parts of a greater network, their cohesion (the solid lines) being dependent on the strength of the inter-connections being noticeably greater within the clump than outside it (hence the dashed lines for

Strings

Stars

Cliques

Clumps

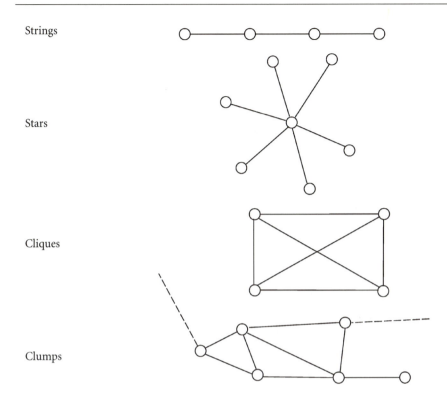

Figure 1. Four types of link between KW nodes (Jones 1971:56 adapted)

external linkages). Thus in formal terms strings, stars and cliques stand alone while clumps link weakly to other parts of a larger network.

Jones points out that these are simple abstractions based on a much more messy and complex network, but they are useful as a means of understanding the basic patterns and possibilities. "Strings and stars are based on individual objects, while cliques and clumps are set-based; ... strings, stars and cliques impose absolute conditions on class membership, while clumps are relatively defined" (1971:56).

We may now hypothesise that a KW plot such as the ones we saw in the previous chapter could be redrawn as a network of connections consisting of configurations reminiscent of strings, stars, cliques and clumps of which the next figure shows a fragment.

This fragment shows one of each type of configuration linked loosely (by dashed lines) into a network, plus a node at the bottom right corner, marked A, a singleton KW which is not part of one of the other 4 configurations. Strictly

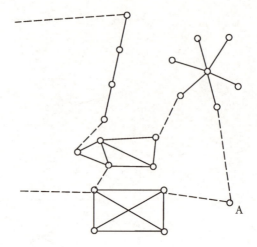

Figure 2. A KW linkage network

speaking, these configurations can only be "reminiscent of" stars, strings or cliques, of course, since in this figure they are weakly connected within a larger "night sky".

The distinction between a dashed line and a solid one must be based on some threshold value determining strength of connection. For example, the connection between *Romeo* and *O* is stronger than that between *Romeo* and *Juliet* in Table 6 of Chapter 4. It is stronger in that table only in simple absolute terms, that is to say because they are found together more often within the same span of 5 words. In the following table of that chapter the connection between *Romeo* and *Juliet* fell below the threshold.

The fragment visible in the figure above represents linkages within a given text, but the formalism does not restrict us to this. It could equally well represent KWs linked between texts, or a combination of within and between. Nothing in the network itself imposes barriers between one text and others.

It is important to realise that the contextual scopes of Figure 2 in Chapter 1 merely represent alternative ways of considering a given "chunk", whatever that chunk may be. The division between scope 6 (the whole text) and scope 5 (the section or chapter) is a matter of agreement, of social convention. For example, the authorship of a given episode of a soap opera like *Coronation Street* need not be the same as that of the next episode. What one person calls a separate text might be part of a continuing text to another. The next division (7, the colony of texts) or 8 (related texts) is determined by such things as the relationships between different journalists and the role of sub-editors and editors in placing articles or boxes on a related page. So in principle there is no reason why we could not consider the above figure simply as a representation of links between KWs without being concerned (except for some practical reason) with whether the lines in question, be they solid or dashed, cross the various scope boundaries discussed in Chapter 1. This also means that it becomes possible to operate research into KW linkage at various scope levels.

Examples of Keyword linkage between texts

For the present, let us, however, operate at the level of scope 6, the whole text, and scopes 7 or 8. This is convenient if the text files on a disk are arranged such that one file is one text. A first procedure is to compute the KWs of a large set, and this was done for the whole of the BNC, spoken and written. The standard default settings for WordSmith were used, namely a minimum of 3 occurrences of each KW, and Dunning's Log Likelihood statistic (Dunning 1993; Oakes 1998: 172) with a p value of 0.000001. A database was then constructed based on the KW files, with the requirement that to be included each text must have a minimum of 10 and a maximum of 500 KWs, and that each KW in the database must appear in at least 5 of the BNC texts. This resulted in a "key word database" of 3,922 KW datasets.

The research questions which interest us here are these:

- Which are the KWs which are linked across texts?
- What sort of a picture of those texts do they paint? Do they reflect the aboutness of the texts, as KWs typically do?

Table 1 shows the most frequently linked ones, the so-called "key key words" (KKWs).

Thus the KW *you* is key in 30% of the BNC. It occurs nearly half a million times, as is shown in the rightmost column.

The first conclusion from looking at this proposed set of KKWs is that a KKW is not so very different from an ordinary word. The top of the list is very reminiscent of the frequency list we saw in Chapter 2, when we were not filtering words by their keyness. Let us examine the bottom of the list organised by frequency in texts.

Table 2 shows that our database contains over 20 thousand KWs, and that the least frequent came in only 5 texts, and with fairly low frequencies in those 5 texts. The last item, *ZX*, appears 49 times in the whole BNC. More precisely, it appears 49 times as a KW in the texts which have at least 10 KWs in the

Table 1. Top 20 KKWs from BNC

KW	Texts	%	Overall Freq.
YOU	1,203	30.00	464,753
I	1,088	27.00	536,462
#	1,039	26.00	1,151,427
OF	948	24.00	1,487,245
THE	915	23.00	2,478,450
WAS	866	22.00	491,050
THAT	841	21.00	384,767
IS	838	21.00	495,330
IT	837	21.00	361,002
WE	787	20.00	155,622
IT'S	755	19.00	86,519
HE	738	18.00	390,984
WHAT	720	18.00	108,707
HIS	670	17.00	256,698
AND	666	16.00	711,403
ARE	651	16.00	208,519
ER	640	16.00	86,609
HAD	627	15.00	243,929
YOUR	620	15.00	84,513
THINK	617	15.00	50,537

corpus. (It is used in formulae and names of machines e.g. cars, printers and components such as computer chips and can be found 65 times in the whole BNC as a word as opposed to a KW.)

It is very likely that the distribution of such KWs is akin to that of words in general, with a small number of high-frequency closed-set items at the top and a very large tail of low frequency items. (The middle item in the list, that is word 10,902, is *spinach*, with a frequency of 12 texts and an overall frequency of 110 instances as a KW in the BNC.)

A KW is an ordinary word which happens to be key in a particular text, as we saw in the last chapter. A KKW, on the other hand, is one which is key in lots of texts, where "lots" is defined (subjectively) by the number of texts in the database. In our present case where there are nearly 4,000 texts, a KKW would be one which occurs in say, 5% or more of the texts. Accordingly, the following tables show the last few KKWs in the database.

The top 290 items in our list, then, represent a lot of closed-set items; even at the end of the list we see a pronoun (*herself*), a modal (*must*), a determiner (*some*). Roughly half (some 147 out of 290 = 51%) of the KKWs are closed set; the 143 open set items are listed on page 80 using title case and italics.

Table 2. Bottom 20 KWs in database from BNC

N	KW	Texts	Overall Freq.
21,785	XYZ	5	38
21,786	YACHTING	5	87
21,787	YAK	5	72
21,788	YAKOVLEV	5	66
21,789	YANKEE	5	39
21,790	YAWNED	5	32
21,791	YEARNING	5	37
21,792	YORKER	5	26
21,793	YORKIST	5	54
21,794	YOURSELVES	5	45
21,795	ZAL	5	49
21,796	ZANU	5	41
21,797	ZEALANDERS	5	32
21,798	ZEEBRUGGE	5	33
21,799	ZION	5	35
21,800	ZIONIST	5	48
21,801	ZIPPED	5	47
21,802	ZOOLOGICAL	5	76
21,803	ZOOS	5	61
21,804	ZX	5	49

Table 3. Last 10 KKWs

N	KW	Texts	%	Overall Freq.
281	YESTERDAY	201	5.00	13,601
282	GOD	200	5.00	12,521
283	HERSELF	200	5.00	10,395
284	NOTHING	200	5.00	9,122
285	ALSO	199	5.00	21,990
286	MUST	199	5.00	16,616
287	WOMEN	199	5.00	17,909
288	CHURCH	198	5.00	12,234
289	SOME	198	5.00	24,997
290	THEREFORE	198	5.00	7,706

Sorting was done by simply examining each KKW and is not claimed to be fully accurate. For example, *love* was classified as a noun, but could very well have represented cases in the source texts where it was a verb.[2]

In answer to our first question, then, the KKWs seem to be dominated by high-frequency closed-set items. In answer to the second, they tell us little about the texts' aboutness. These 143 open-set KKWs above may provide some

Table 4. KKW nouns

84 Nouns

Bed, Bit, Business, Car, Case, Century, Chapter, Children, Church, Committee, Community, Companies, Company, Computer, Council, Course, Court, Data, Development, Door, Example, Eyes, Face, Family, Father, God, Government, Group, Head, Health, Home, House, Industry, Information, John, Life, London, Lord, Lot, Love, Man, Management, Market, Members, Men, Money, Mother, Night, Nothing, Party, People, Police, Policy, Power, Products, Report, Room, Sales, School, Service, Services, Society, Something, Sort, Staff, State, Support, System, Systems, Team, Technology, Thing, Things, Trade, Training, Uk, War, Water, Week, Woman, Women, Work, World, Year

Table 5. KKW verbs

28 Verbs

Act, Asked, Came, Come, Felt, Get, Go, Knew, Know, Like, Look, Looked, Mean, Need, Put, Said, Sat, Say, Says, Tell, Think, Thought, Told, Turned, Use, Used, Want, Went

Table 6. KKW adverbs and adjectives

6 Adverbs

Actually, Just, Never, Really, Well, Yesterday

25 Adjectives

Available, Based, British, Different, East, Economic, European, General, Good, International, Labour, Last, Little, Local, National, New, Old, Particular, Political, Public, Right, Social, South, Therefore, Twenty

kind of indication as to what BNC texts are often about, but because it is relatively frequent (the least frequent comes as a KW in 198 BNC texts), each one is fairly general in meaning, so it cannot really be claimed that KKWs provide a *good* indication of aboutness in the BNC. The 28 verbs and the 6 adverbs in particular do not seem to tell us what was being said. The adjectives and nouns do give some idea, but nowhere near as convincingly as the KWs of individual texts we saw in the last chapter.

So far we have been considering the KKWs of a whole corpus based on both spoken and written text and a variety of genres. Let us now narrow down somewhat. Table 7 shows the top 25 KKWs of the two separate modes of the BNC.

These items are well within our "key key" threshold – the 50th item of the spoken column, *very*, is key in 26% of the spoken texts and the 50th written text KKW, *looked*, is key in 10%. The right column is very similar to that of the whole BNC, which is hardly surprising given that 90% of the BNC is writ-

Table 7. Top 25 KKWs in BNC spoken and written

Spoken	Written
YOU	#
ER	OF
I	THE
IT'S	WAS
ERM	IS
THAT'S	HIS
THAT	HE
THINK	ARE
IT	HAD
GOT	HAS
WHAT	IN
KNOW	WILL
WELL	AND
DO	BY
WE	YOU
YES	OR
SO	HIM
YEAH	I
JUST	BE
RIGHT	ITS
DON'T	WHICH
GET	HER
I'M	WERE
MEAN	SAID
THERE'S	ME

ten text. The KKWs of the left column are much more reminiscent of spoken language, with hesitations (*er, erm*), one word comments/answers (*OK, No, Oh* are within the top 50), etc. However, we still do not find *good* indicators of the aboutness of the spoken corpus texts, of which there were 851 meeting the database criteria described above.

Let us now narrow down somewhat more, by genre. The following table shows KKWs where the database was constructed using Lee's (2001) identification of the genres in the BNC, formally embedded in the header codes of each BNC World edition text, separating the written academic from all other written texts. In this table and in several which follow, we will use lower case to mark closed set items, and again use *Title case italics* for open set items. Items are in order of key keyness.

Table 8. Top 50 KKWs in BNC written academic & non-academic text

Non-academic
#, was, his, the, he, had, of, has, will, you, is, him, I, and, said, her, are, me, she, its, your, *New*, my, *Year*, at, back, by, in, were, it, a, *Looked*, *Man*, *Company*, up, or, our, would, but, we, *Like*, down, out, to, be, who, *Knew*, *Room*, *Eyes*, *Mr*

Academic
of, the, is, in, which, #, such, by, or, be, are, between, these, this, as, that, may, *Case*, *Example*, *Social*, *Act*, *However*, *Thus*, *C*, not, *Particular*, *Court*, *E*, *B*, *Analysis*, their, *Chapter*, *Evidence*, to, *Section*, *Different*, *Cases*, *V*, an, were, *Groups*, *Terms*, *Law*, non, *Order*, within, *Therefore*, *Appeal*, *L*, can, *T*

This broad distinction between academic and non-academic, like the spoken/written distinction, does not yet pull out many KKWs telling us about the aboutness of the texts.

Let us now consider a set of 5 genres within the overall academic category. The following table shows the top KKWs in Academic Humanities, Medicine, Natural Science, Politics-Law-Education and Technology-and-Engineering texts (Table 9).

These KKWs are more promising. It is still clear that some closed-set items appear near the top of the list but the typical aboutness of the texts is beginning to appear. The Medical texts are probably those where this aboutness is most visible, and the Humanities texts the least clear in this regard. In Natural Science there are also visible KKWs which relate to the text itself (e.g. *fig.*, *figure*, *shown*).

Let us check whether this pattern holds with the same database domains (Academic Humanities, Medicine, Natural Science, Politics-Law-Education and Technical-and-Engineering) but using the non-academic variant (Table 10).

The same basic pattern in the KKWs is visible in the non-academic genres. Aboutness is much more clearly attained as the genre becomes domain-specific. There are still some closed-set items characterising the style and not the content, but they have become a small minority.

There are also some interesting features of the different lists. The Medical texts focus less on the process of studying than on the treatment and cure; Sciences and Technology move away from the research procedure too. In the case of Technology and Engineering we see more company and product names, in the Natural Sciences the term *scientist(s)* comes to the fore, as in popular science's typical references to "scientists believe", "scientists characterise dolphins by..." etc.

Table 9. Top academic KKWs by domain

Humanities
of, the, in, which, as, is, *Century*, by, was, were, between, its, *Political*, this, such, that, *Sense*, his, are, or, *Early*, *War*, *Seems*, their, *Theory*, *Thus*, an, *Tradition*, and, *Evidence*, itself, *Literary*, *Military*, not, *Terms*, *Contemporary*, even, had, *II*, *Nature*, *Religious*, these, *World*, *Argument*, be, *However*, might, rather, *Text*, *Cultural*

Medicine
Clinical, *Patients*, *Treatment*, *Patient*, *Disease*, of, *Study*, *Diagnosis*, *Incidence*, *Results*, *Studies*, #, *Non*, *Reported*, *Risk*, *Symptoms*, *Analysis*, *Associated*, *Chronic*, *Data*, in, *Increased*, *Prevalence*, *Significant*, *Acute*, *Compared*, *Findings*, *Group*, *Medical*, *Surgery*, these, with, *Age*, *Care*, *Cases*, *Groups*, *Hospital*, *Severe*, *Significantly*, were, *Concentrations*, *Dose*, *Health*, *Infection*, between, *Blood*, *Concentration*, *Effects*, *Mg*, *Mortality*

Natural Science
#, are, *C*, *Fig*, *Shown*, is, *Figure*, of, *Regions*, *B*, by, *Region*, *M*, *Observed*, *Sequence*, *Containing*, *Corresponding*, *E*, *N*, *Obtained*, *Surface*, *Using*, *Analysis*, *G*, *Present*, *Species*, *T*, *Temperature*, these, which, *Derived*, *H*, in, may, *Sequences*, the, *DNA*, *Gene*, *Genes*, *Similar*, *Sites*, *X*, *Cell*, *Data*, *Form*, *Fragments*, *Indicated*, *Occur*, *P*, *Protein*

Politics, Law, Education
the, of, *Court*, *Act*, #, or, *Case*, which, be, *V*, *Appeal*, by, *Judgment*, that, such, *Section*, is, to, under, *Law*, *C*, *L*, whether, *Order*, not, *R*, *B*, any, may, *Proceedings*, in, an, *Courts*, *Decision*, *Authority*, *Cases*, *J*, *E*, *Circumstances*, should, *Defendant*, *Person*, *Judge*, *Evidence*, *Legal*, *Lord*, *Ltd*, *Lords*, *Provisions*, *Property*

Technology & Engineering
is, be, *Example*, are, each, can, *E*, such, this, *Using*, #, of, *Required*, *Systems*, the, *Values*, *Data*, *Method*, *Number*, *System*, *Thus*, *Components*, *Form*, *Information*, *Input*, *Level*, *Possible*, *Process*, *Section*, these, *Use*, *Used*, *B*, *Described*, *N*, *Output*, *Program*, *Representation*, *Value*, above, *Algorithm*, *Analysis*, *Chapter*, *Computer*, *Corresponding*, *Current*, *G*, may, *Nodes*, *Problem*

In conclusion, we can decide that for this corpus taken *as a whole*, KKWs do not contain many open-set items which are informative about the aboutness of the texts in each division of the corpus; that on the contrary the KKW distribution is akin to an ordinary word frequency distribution. On the other hand, when the corpus is broken down by domain, we conclude that KKWs are informative of aboutness, and to a much lesser degree, of style. This conclusion is an important modification of work such as Scott (1997a, 1997b) based on newspaper features texts, where my analysis of KKWs led me to believe (and choose a term suggesting) that the top KWs in a database are generally even more "key" than key words, because they are key of many of the texts in the database. Such a general conclusion can now be seen to be false. It is true only if the genre in question is quite specific.

Table 10. Top 50 KKWs in 5 BNC written non-academic genres

Humanities
the, of, was, were, by, in, *Century*, had, his, *War*, and, *Became*, which, as, #, their, *Church, Great*, its, *Later, Men, William*, who, is, *King, Ancient, Early*, at, *Power, St, Building, Built, John, Land, London, Nineteenth, Roman, South, Thus, Town, Centuries, East, Empire, North, Period, Political, Remained, Royal*, among, *Army*

Medicine
or, can, is, are, be, may, *Body, Help, Patient, Patients, Cause, Disease, Health*, if, *Infection, Medical, Pain, Physical, Treatment*, will, your, and, *Care, Drugs, Feel, Food, Need, Often, Patient's, Stress, Symptoms, Usually*, you, *Blood, Breathing, Difficult, Diseases, Hospital, Learn, Loss*, many, *Muscles, Normal, Nurse, Nurses, People, Problems, Required*, these, this

Natural Science
of, is, the, are, *Scientists, Cells, Scientific, Energy*, its, *Research, Chemical, Science, Million, Technology, Animals, Molecules, Species, Atoms, Surface, Water, Cell, Particles*, can, *Carbon, Electron, Nuclear, Animal, Experiments*, has, *New, Solar, Human, Laboratory, Radiation, Scientist*, that, *Genetic, Molecular, Per*, such, *University, Cent, DNA, Earth, Electrons, Gas, Oxygen, Physics, Plants, Researchers*

Politics, Law, Education
of, *Political*, the, *Party, Government, Economic*, had, *Union, National*, #, by, *Election*, in, *State*, were, *Cent, Foreign, Parties, Defence, Democratic, Europe, Members, Military, Minister, Ministers, Per, Countries, Leaders, Soviet, States, Trade, Army, Leader, Republic, Secretary, Communist, Constitution, Constitutional, East, Parliament, Prime, Coalition, Elected, Forces, Agreement, Assembly, Cabinet, Congress, Elections, General*

Technology & Engineering
#, *Systems, Software, Based, Computer, Corp, Ibm, Inc*, its, *System, Technology, Company, Unix, Says*, will, *Users, Applications*, has, *Server, Network, Microsoft, Products, Corp's, Hewlett, Ltd, Data, Packard, Inc's, Operating, Quarter, Version, Windows, Intel, Interface, Co, Microsystems, Desktop, Risc, Market, Chip, Nt, Sun, California, Digital, Database, User, Servers, Hardware, Distributed, Machines*

The tendency discussed here also leads to testable predictions, e.g. for any suitable corpus[3]

1. a set of KKWs based on the whole corpus will be akin to an ordinary word frequency list in favouring a few very high-frequency closed-set items and an enormous tail of very low-frequency open-set items; it will not be informative of the aboutness of the corpus;
2. a set of KKWs based on a suitable genre[4] and representing a small section of the corpus will have many more open-set items informative of aboutness and far fewer closed-set items;
3. any closed-set items in the case of prediction 2 will be indicative of style.

Associates

With a KW database covering hundreds or thousands of texts, it becomes possible to consider the notion of KWs which link across texts. If co-keyness is shared keyness in the same text, as defined above, "**associates**" are *the set of words which are co-key with a given KW-node across a range of texts*. That is, if we take a KKW which is found in a number of texts and then determine all the set of co-key items in all those texts, we get associates.

The following example is of the associates of *time* in the BNC's commerce texts. The first 25 words which share keyness within the 12 texts where *time* is key are these. It is clear that in the commercial world time is presented as something which has to be organised and managed.

In the following study, three overall BNC domains, Humanities, Politics-Law-Education, Technology-Engineering were selected. For each of these do-

Table 11. Associates of *time* in BNC Commerce texts

Commerce texts, associates of "TIME"
FLOW
ORGANIZATION
JOB
RISK
CHAPTER
SAMPLE
PROFIT
MUST
PROJECTS
DESIGN
RESPONSIBILITY
SPECIFIC
CONTRACTS
SELLING
COMPANY'S
DECISIONS
QUALITY
INFORMATION
PAY
TERMS
ASSETS
MANAGEMENT
EACH
WILL
CONTRACT

mains two KKW databases were computed, one of the non-academic variety and the other of the academic.

Tables 12–14 show the top 25 associates in each of the 6 KKW databases, preceded by the number of texts in which each KKW appeared as a KW[5] and the total number of texts in the database.

For the KKW *century*, we get a number of well-defined periods (17th, 18th, 19th) for the non-academic but possibly less specific ones in the academic texts.

Table 12. Associates of *Century* in Humanities

Humanities	
"CENTURY"	
Non-Academic 50/111	Academic 39/87
Church, were, by, *Nineteenth, William, Became, Great, Centuries, Medieval, Roman,* was, *Reign, John, Later, Ancient, Eighteenth, Buildings, Early,* in, of, *Thomas, King, St, Built, Seventeenth*	*Early,* were, *Religious, Period,* by, between, *Military, War, Tradition, Reign,* which, *Political, Evidence,* was, *Lands, English, II,* in, *Imperial, Centuries, Sources,* of, *Empire,* his, *King*

Table 13. Associates of *Court* in Politics, Law, Education .

Politics, Law, Education	
"COURT"	
Non-Academic 13/93	Academic 111/186
Resigned, Declared, Palestinian, Parliament, Voted, Resignation, Officials, Americas, Deputies, Reportedly, Referendum, Deputy, Secretary, Yeltsin, Israeli, Ministers, Pacific, Privatization, Asia, Iranian, China, Multiparty, Leaders, Force, Constitutional	*Appeal, Judgment, Act, Case, V, Section, C, L, Proceedings, R,* under, *B, Order,* whether, *J, Judge, Courts, Defendant, Law,* any, *E, Lord, Circumstances, Ltd, Lords*

Table 14. Associates of *Systems* in Technology & Engineering

Technology & Engineering	
"SYSTEMS"	
Non-Academic 119/123	Academic 13/23
IBM, Computer, Technology, Based, Corp, Software, Company, Inc, Users, Server, System, Says, Applications, Network, Microsoft, Corp's, Hewlett, Products, Unix, Packard, Ltd, its, *Inc's, Operating, Data*	*Required, Using, System,* each, *Approach, Example, Level,* such, *Information, Techniques, Components, Stored, Number, Analysis, Processing, Current, Process, Possible, Data, E, Computer, Structures, Types, Representation, Shows*

In the case of the academic Politics-Law-Education we see a lot of specific terms to do with court cases while the non-academic ones are concerned with wider political implications.

The non-academic technology set seems to be concerned much more with products than the admittedly small academic variety where there seems to be more emphasis on procedure.

The tables are interesting as an example of what could be done, not as a definitive listing of reliable differences between KW associates. That is because the number of texts in each of the six databases is limited. In the case of the academic technology and engineering database there are only 23 texts. Moreover, there is no guarantee – or likelihood – that the academic and non-academic sets deal with the same issues; for that a more specific corpus than the BNC would be needed.

Nevertheless it is clear that this notion, associates, and the database technology bring with them potential access to a wealth of related terms which could have important implications for the study and learning of vocabulary. This is further developed in Scott (2002) where linkage patterns are discussed in a database of 0.8 million texts all from the same source.

The picture here is not necessarily of established linkage between items like *church* and *century* or *systems* and *approach*, or *appeal* and *court*. In some cases (*appeal* and *court* might well be one) the linkage is phraseological and builds up a multi-word unit, and this can be established by significantly frequent re-occurrence in a large set of texts. In others what we are accessing is stereotype. That is, the linkages created within and between texts are not claimed to be other than what writers decide to say, and what they choose to tell us is not at all the same as what co-occurs in real life. (For example, all elephants have lungs, but very few texts choose to say so. What we say about elephants is more typically concerned with ivory, poaching etc.)

Conclusion

This chapter has been mostly concerned with keyword linkage. We started with a formal system for thinking about links and we ended up with the notion of associates. It is still too early to be sure where this powerful notion will lead.

Notes

1. Incidentally this procedure was criticised by Charolles (1989:40) as "intuitive, how could it be justified?"

2. It would be possible to re-compute all the database using POS-marked words as with the study in the last chapter.

3. Suitable to generate enough KWs to build a database, and using a relevant reference corpus (see Chapter 4). This probably means a corpus containing at least one thousand texts.

4. Suitable here must mean determined not by KW analysis but by some other procedure as discussed by Lee (2001), presumably based, at least in part, on external criteria such as having its text labelled as domain-specific by the author or a human reader.

5. Naturally each KKW could appear in other texts without being key in them, e.g. in incidental mentions.

PART II

## CHAPTER 6

General English language teaching

Grammar and lexis in spoken and written texts

Summary

In this chapter we will show how an analysis of small collections of texts which deal with similar content (but which are the result of spoken interactions or writing) can help teachers and students to come to an appreciation of the contrasting linguistic choices speakers and writers make in the process of producing these texts.

We will use the grammatical and lexical differences between spoken and written language as the starting point for this analysis (Halliday 1989, 1994; Biber et al. 2000) and show how small scale corpus resources can offer teachers and students practical ways of getting a better understanding of this contrast. Sophisticated corpus analysis methods have been used to demonstrate this variation across speaking and writing (Biber 1988; Lee 2001), but it is impractical for most teachers to try to replicate this kind of exhaustive statistical study. KW analysis, however, is an approach which is suitable for research and pedagogy, and gives teachers and learners an accessible means for building an understanding of variation across large or small collections of texts.

During this discussion we will model a systematic approach to using corpus resources in text analysis, and show ways in which findings from such analyses can be used in language study. Subsequent chapters will build on the techniques exemplified here to provide more detailed accounts of how KW analysis can be of value to teachers, students or other researchers interested in specific areas of language use.

Introduction

Up until now, large scale corpus resources like the British National Corpus and the COBUILD Bank of English have been used by lexicographers (Rundell

2002; Summers 1987; Sinclair 1987), and grammarians (e.g. Sinclair 1990; Biber et al. 2000) to develop accounts of spoken and written variation. In this process, they have provided learners of English with opportunities to gain an enhanced understanding of the ways in which the resources of the language are used in contrasting ways, depending on the context in which the language is being used.

In contrast to these large scale studies, Biber (1990) has demonstrated the value of small corpora such as the 1 million word LOB (Lancaster Oslo Bergen) corpus in the development of practical accounts of the grammar of a language.

While such reference works and studies of small balanced corpora provide important insights, we would argue that there is also significant value in foreign language learners undertaking their own investigations into smaller and more specialised text collections – especially as they develop in their ability to operate in the L2 and need to gain a greater understanding of how language use changes in response to contextual constraints. Such a point is arrived at when students begin to use the target language for study purposes, and in so doing start to encounter the rhetorical and textual conventions associated with the disciplines they wish to enter as apprentice writers. While those studying in their mother tongue can also find this experience daunting, learners working in a foreign language – especially those whose earlier learning experiences have emphasised spoken interaction – can encounter major problems when beginning to write for advanced academic or professional purposes.

In such a context, this chapter has two functions. First we will show how text-oriented (and often small scale) corpus analysis can give teachers and foreign language students insights into lexico-grammatical contrasts between spoken and written production. We will do this through the examination of four small sets of exemplar texts:[1]

– examples of academic writing from disciplines represented in the BNC
– examples of academic spoken texts from the same discipline areas
– examples of unplanned conversation
– prose fiction texts

Second, we will model a process of exploration which we use in our own approach to language study and which others may find useful in investigations in their own fields.

Table 1. Resources

Written Academic texts	**6 examples**	226,520 words
	History	
	Social Science	
	Political Science	
	Medical Science	
	Natural Science	
	Engineering	
Spoken Academic texts	**5 examples**	34,885 words
	History	
	Social Science	
	Political Science	
	Natural Science	
	Engineering	
Fiction texts	**2 examples**	64,297 words
Conversational Production	**115 examples**	170,850 words

Resources

The resources used in this chapter are the following:

a. 15 texts taken from BNC World Edition 2000 (Total words: 497,182)
b. Dave Lee's BNC Index (Lee 2001) – an invaluable guide to the texts included in the BNC
c. Three computer programs running under Microsoft Windows XP:

- Wordsmith Tools (Scott 1996a)
- Microsoft Word
- Microsoft Excel

Approach

The texts chosen for this chapter have been selected in order to represent a range of contexts of production (and interpretation), and because the written texts are identified in the BNC index as being complete. Set 1 (Written – academic) covers the six BNC academic writing genre categories identified by Lee (Lee 2001); Set 2, the five spoken academic genres (there is no medical lecture text in the corpus); Set 3, two prose fiction examples; and Set 4, two sets of unplanned conversations. We consider these texts as occupying positions on a cline extending from those more likely to be typical of formal, planned written production, and those more likely to be typical of informal, unplanned spoken conversation.

The issue which concerns us is that of assessing the extent to which it is possible to use KW analysis as a means of identifying and building a pedagogically useful account of contrasts within and between these small text sets. Our assumption is that it will be relatively trivial – though nevertheless valuable – to distinguish between individual texts on the basis of the patterning of content lexis, but that it will also be possible to distinguish between texts arising from spoken and written contexts (academic written / academic spoken / prose fiction / conversational) on the basis of *non*-content lexical patterning – and that this information will be more interesting.

Procedure

The basic methodology for KW analysis will be the same for all the following chapters in this section of the book. We present it here in some detail, but will not repeat this account unless there are significant differences in later preparatory stages.

Step 1 – Select texts

In this instance, Lee's BNC Index was used to identify texts which arose from similar academic domains and contexts of production, or which shared similar genre spaces (i.e. conversation / prose fiction). Texts in the BNC source – stored locally on a hard drive – were searched for by file name (using Windows Explorer) and copied to a separate folder. Each file was then given a meaningful prefix to allow for easier processing.

Step 2 – Make wordlists

Wordlists for each text set were made using Wordsmith tools. When generating the wordlists, Wordsmith Tools was set to ignore tags - thereby excluding the BNC POS tags.[2] Wordlists were all saved using file names which could be easily related to the data files.

Step 3 – Make Keyword lists

Two keyword lists for each file were made, using reference wordlists taken from contrasting one million word corpora (BNC Sampler Written / BNC Sampler Spoken). As we have seen in Chapter 5 it can be advantageous to use this approach in KW analysis as it often provides a much richer account of the texts being studies, and brings out contrasting aspects of a text or a text collection.

Step 4 – Save lists as text files

All keyword and key-keyword lists were then saved as text files. This step is important as you cannot import Wordsmith's native file format into other programs (e.g. spreadsheets or Microsoft Word® tables).

Step 5 – Create an Excel workbook containing all the data

Wordlists were then imported into a Microsoft Excel® workbook. This is easily done by opening each text file in Excel, and then using the *Edit, Move or Copy Sheet* feature. The final workbook had 32 sheets devoted to the individual BNC files, eight keyword files for Spoken Academic, Conversational Production, Written Academic, Fiction (referenced against both BNC sampler spoken and written), four key-keyword sheets for the same text sets, and five key-keyword sheets for those domains which were represented in both the spoken and the written sections of the BNC (humanities, natural sciences, political science, social science, technology and engineering). The example below (Figure 1) shows a section of the resulting spreadsheet for a spoken academic humanities file.

Findings

The volume of data represented by the lists obtained through this KW analysis is quite daunting. In order to draw out the contrasts between the different sets – and to give the reader a better chance of seeing the method in our madness, we will begin by looking at an extreme contrast – that between edited written production and unplanned conversation. We will then compare the intermediate cases we have included in the study: spoken academic texts and fiction.

	A	B	C	D	E	F	G	H
1	N	CONTENT	FUNCTION	FREQ.	SA HUF.T	FREQ.	CORPUS	KEYNESS
2	1		ERM	66	0.8	9		591.1
3	2	MILL		63	0.77	7		571.2
4	3	DEMOCRACY		57	0.69	72		381.9
5	4	PEOPLE		108	1.31	1,112	0.1	344.4
6	5	VOTE		53	0.64	208	0.02	258.4
7	6		THAT	227	2.76	8,803	0.81	235.7
8	7		SO	106	1.29	1,925	0.18	234.4
9	8		ER	32	0.39	29		229.1
10	9	THINKS		28	0.34	44		178.4
11	10		WE	111	1.35	3,280	0.3	158.6

Cell reference: B35 = OBJECTION. Sheet tabs: sahuf_pol, saj8k_natsc, sajp6_tech, sakrj_soc, s...

Figure 1. Keyword spreadsheet

Written academic vs. conversation

The first analysis deals with text collections at opposite poles of a spoken –
written continuum. In line with Halliday's 1989 comments on the orientation
of written production towards facts and spoken production towards interaction and relationship building, a review of the results of KW analysis on the
basis of contrasts between frequencies of content and function words offers
few surprises. For these purposes we take *content words* to be those which refer
to "a thing, quality, state or action and which have meaning when the words
are used alone" (Richards et al. 1985:61) and *function words* are those which
"have little meaning on their own but which show grammatical relationships
in and between sentences" (Richards et al. 1985:61).

As you will see in Table 2, 18 out of the top 20 keywords in Written Academic are content words (referenced against BNC Written). The analysis of
Conversational Production provides almost a mirror image, with 18 out of 20
keywords being function words – the majority of which are implicated in the
maintenance of interaction.

The table demonstrates the way in which KW analysis lays bare the contrast between a research collection and the original reference corpus. The texts
in Written Academic have particularly narrowly focused topics, so when they
are compared with a balanced sample of written texts (such as BNC sampler
written) topic related words like *patients*, *species*, and *democracy* will be found
at the top of the list. A KW analysis of the collection of unplanned conversa-

Table 2. Written Academic vs. Conversational Production referenced against BNC Written

	Written Academic (ref. BNC Written)	Conversational Production (ref. BNC Written)
1.	PATIENTS	YEAH
2.	SPECIES	YOU
3.	DEMOCRACY	I
4.	**OF**	N'T
5.	INPUT	IT
6.	IMPEDANCE	OH
7.	SIGNAL	S
8.	FOREST	DO
9.	CIRCUIT	GOT
10.	EQUATION	KNOW
11.	FREQUENCY	WELL
12.	FILTER	ER
13.	FIGURE	MM
14.	SEEDS	NO
15.	RESISTANCE	VE
16.	PHASE	WHAT
17.	OUTPUT	THAT
18.	**THAT**	COS
19.	CONSERVATIVE	NA
20.	TROPICAL	ERM

tions in Conversational Production, in contrast, quite logically foregrounds a completely different set of vocabulary – *yeah*, *you*, *I*, and the like.

Written Academic has strong factual orientation / Conversational Production focuses on interaction. Also, again obviously, the keyword list for Written Academic gives a strong indication of the themes that are important in the texts in the text collection. Less obviously, If we focus on the function words in the list, we also gain a strong indication of the communicative purposes of the texts in the Written Academic collection – and the language forms necessary to achieving those purposes.

If this is the case when our contrasting text collections are compared with a larger selection of written texts, what happens when we run a KW analysis referenced against spoken language?

On first viewing, we might think that there are few differences between the two sets of results – *species, patients, democracy* are still high in the Written Academic list, and *yeah* and *n't* are still there in the top five for Conversational Production. However, a closer review shows important and possibly surprising

Table 3. Written Academic vs. Conversational Production (eferenced against BNC Spoken)

Written Academic (ref. BNC Spoken)	Conversational Production (ref. BNC Spoken)
OF	YEAH
THE	N'T
BY	ANN
IN	YOU
SPECIES	NO
PATIENTS	I
DEMOCRACY	BLOODY
GOVERNMENT	OH
SUCH	IT
INPUT	STUART
FOREST	ALRIGHT
SIGNAL	S
FIGURE	FIFTEEN
ITS	GOT
FREQUENCY	DO
AS	WELL
IMPEDANCE	HA
RESISTANCE	RICKY
CIRCUIT	HELL
OUTPUT	MORTGAGE

differences. In Written Academic, *of, the, by* and *in* are now the top five keywords. In Conversational Production we find that *Ann* has entered the top five, and now only 11 out of the keyword 20 top are function words, although the discourse maintenance terms are still prominent.

By using a different reference corpus for this second study (a collection of spoken texts) a different kind of contrast between Written Academic and Conversational Production has been brought out; one that needs some explaining. A more detailed account of *of* – a keyword in Written Academic irrespective of which reference corpus was used – will demonstrate one of the major contrasts between written and spoken language revealed by the KW analysis. A study of *that* – a keyword in Written Academic and Conversational Production – when referenced against BNC Written, will demonstrate other systematic contrasts between the two modes of language production.

Of

Although it would not be surprising to find *of* at the top of a frequency sorted wordlist for an English text – along with THE it tends to be one of the most frequent words in any text – *of* is worth commenting on when it is found in a keyword list – i.e. is statistically prominent in the source texts when compared against a general population. Sinclair (Sinclair 1991) has commented on the status of *of* as a preposition, preferring to see it as a partitive participle and best viewed as an element in terms of the noun which it follows, rather than the noun it precedes. This becomes significant when we take into account what Halliday (1989) describes as the *lexical density* of written production. In brief, the argument runs that:

1. texts associated with administrative or academic institutions – where the reporting or recording of factual information and the development of arguments is the main concern – tend to be rich in nouns, and
2. where information is concentrated in thematised noun phrases, there is a strong tendency to find more noun phrase elaboration – especially by post-modification (most commonly with of-phrases, participles or relatives).

We can hypothesise that there are lots of instances of *of* in Written Academic, because there are lots of information rich noun phrases. An initial test of this argument can be made by using the POS information in BNC. In Wordsmith it is possible to count POS tags – in this case we looked for NN1, singular noun, and NN2, plural noun. The following results in Table 4 were obtained.

Table 4 shows clearly that in terms of rank (e.g. Written Academic: NN1 = 1 / Conversational Production: NN1 = 10), normalised counts per thousand, and percentage there are proportionally many more nouns in the written text than there are in the spoken.

A concordance on *of* as it is used in Written Academic adds further support for the argument. Table 5 summarises an analysis of *of* in Written Academic

Table 4. Nouns in Written Academic and Conversational Production

Rank	Noun	Nouns per thousand words	% of total words
Written academic			
1	Singular	188.02	5.3
8	Plural	68.97	1.94
Conv. production			
10	Singular	84.71	1.69
40	Plural	16.71	0.33

Table 5. Noun + *of* (Written Academic vs. Conversational Production)

	TOTAL Words	Total "*of*"	Normalised (counts per thousand)	<w nn*	%
W	228412	9752	42.69	7719	79.15
CP	172445	1625	9.42	791	48.68

and Conversational Production – again using POS information in BNC. As can be seen, the contrast between the two text sets is, once again, marked – whether considered as a raw total or a normalised count. This difference is underscored when the percentage of instances of *of* immediately following a noun (the search string *of in the context of* <NN* catches all instances of preceding nouns) is considered. 79.15% instances of *of* in Written Academic are immediately preceded by a noun as opposed to only 48.68% in Conversational Production.

When these are looked at more closely, we find another significant contrast between Written Academic and Conversational Production – the immediate left collocates[3] of *of* in Conversational Production constitute a very small set of words (listed in Table 6) with the top five *sort, bit, one, lot,* and *out* making up 40% of the total, and the top 20 accounting for 71% of the total instances.

Even where there are instances of post-modifying *of* in Conversational Production, it tends to be in the context of fixed, highly generalised phrases, and spans an extremely small set. In extreme contrast, in Written Academic the top 20 left collocates of *of* constitute a much smaller percentage of the total instances (23% – with the top five only representing 10%).

From a language teaching perspective, this set of collocates of *of* in Written Academic is also significant in that it offers at least two potentially useful insights for learners. The first is that it provides a starting point for a review of the prefabs (see Cowie 2001) that were used by this set of writers (and which are likely to be important for other academic writers). *terms of, range of, form of, case of, principle of, effect of, function of* are all potentially valuable to apprentice writers. Secondly, it could be used as the starting point for even narrower disciplinary investigations of the left collocates of *of*. In the present instance, the list also leads rather neatly to a consideration of *that* – one of the strong left collocates of *of* in Written Academic, and a Written Academic function keyword in its own right.

Table 6. Immediate left collocates of "of" in Conversational Production & immediate left collocates of of in Written Academic

Conversational Production: Total instances of *of*: 1623
Written Academic: Total instances of *of*: 9571

N	WORD	TOTAL	subtotal	WORD	TOTAL	subtotal
1	SORT	178		TERMS	162	
2	BIT	113		ONE	294	
3	ONE	169		PART	116	
4	LOT	101		SPECIES	272	
5	OUT	99	660	NUMBER	104	948
6	SOME	72		RANGE	99	
7	COUPLE	43		SOME	252	
8	PAIR	38		USE	102	
9	CUP	31		THAT	792	
10	END	36		BECAUSE	121	
11	SHOULD	32		FORM	112	
12	BECAUSE	33		CASE	78	
13	INSTEAD	18		IDEA	78	
14	ALL	76		MOST	157	
15	KIND	18		END	67	
16	ANY	33		HISTORY	69	
17	MOST	17		PRINCIPLE	69	
18	PART	21		EFFECT	73	
19	PIECE	20		FUNCTION	68	
20	PLENTY	16		MANY	123	
	TOTAL	1164		TOTAL	2260	

That

That *that* is a keyword in Written Academic, *and* in Conversational Production is also counter-intuitive. Like *of, that* is, generally speaking, a highly frequent word in most texts. In BNC it is #18 in the full BNC, #17 in BNC Written, #15 in the Context Governed sections of BNC Spoken, and #9 in the Demographic section of BNC Spoken.[4] So why should it be a keyword in Written Academic and Conversational Production?

In terms of the statistical engine in Wordsmith, *that* simply forms a significantly higher percentage of the words in Written Academic and Conversational Production than it does in the reference wordlist (Written Academic = 1.23% // Conversational Production = 2.2% // BNC Written 0.81%). Hence, it's a keyword. But this is not the end of the story. If we consider the roles that *that* plays in Written Academic and Conversational Production, we get yet another view of how the language of the two text collections differs – and how writers and speakers draw on different resources to achieve their different ends.

The first two tables (Table 7, Table 8) below show the major distribution of POS categories associated with *that* in the two text collections, and make clear the overwhelming contrast between Written Academic and Conversational Production in the ways in which *that* is used in clause elaboration in Written Academic and in reference to shared knowledge in Conversational Production.

Table 7. *That* POS categories in Written Academic

Written Academic: Total *that* = 2,820 // 1.23% of total words

N	POS tag	POS descriptor	L1	example
1	CJT	subordinating conjunction	1970	On the other hand, it seems implausible \<w CJT>**that** most male English adults readily consented . . .
2	DT0	determiner	639	vote to the working class would give them \<w DT0>**that** sense of citizen responsibility which they were . . .
b3	CJS	subordinating conjunction (relative clause)	152	need to solicit public support \<w CJS>**Provided that** the Cabinet was aware of the company's
4	AV0	Adverb (in adverb phrase)	49	of human knowledge: "technique", \<w AV0>**that** is, skills which can be taught or a

Table 8. *That* POS categories in Conversational Production

Conversational Production: Total *that* = 3,653 // 2.12% of total words

N	POS tag	POS descriptor	L1	example
1	DT0	determiner	2982	a couple of bets in the bookies \<w DT0>**that** sort of thing.
2	CJT	subordinating conjunction	572	Her with the withered paralyzed arm \<w CJT>**that** she bashed you with because she could
3	AV0	Adverb (in adverb phrase)	64	there's not \<w AV0>**that** many there is there?
4	CJS	subordinating conjunction (relative clause)	31	I would prefer an empty property \<w CJS>**so that** when we decide and then whatever just . . .

Specifically, we can say that:

In Written Academic the vast majority of instances of *that* function as subordinating conjunctions – i.e. *that* is primarily deployed in Written Academic to build clause complexes, e.g.:

```
 One outcome of this is   that there is not a single national
ompanies, it is certain   that the media will not accurately r
ciety, and consequently   that there cannot be a properly bala
 important to democracy   that government should be not merely
    has to say. This means   that leaders and government have to
d, given the great gulf   that has opened up between them in s
es, this probably means   that the government has to go to the
```

Figure 2. "That" in written production

In Conversational Production *that* is mainly used as a determiner and often then as a pro-form. In these cases *that* is frequently associated with the exophoric reference typical of conversation, e.g:

```
   one though. </p> <PS02X:> Ah,  that's nice. That's ours are
<PS02Y:> Pull coat down Nee ah,  that's better hate this bit.
S02G:> Yeah. </p> <PS6TB:> Ah,  that come out, that nearly <
I was close! </p> <PS0K8:> Ah,  that's pretty, I'll send off
e the boots. </p> <PS0JY:> Aha, that's what your doing, not
```

Figure 3. "That" in spoken production

The impact of this contrast becomes clear when immediate left collocates of *that* in Written Academic and Conversational Production are compared. In Written Academic, apart from the first five, (*so, and, is, fact, in*) the majority of left collocates are clearly related to the development of arguments, the qualification of opinions and references to authority – core issues in academic discourse.

Given the importance of the issues involve here, a list of verbs extracted from the top 50 collocates of *that* in appropriate narrow spectrum text collections is likely to provide suggestive starting points for EAP vocabulary development. In the present instance we get a list as in Table 10.

The contrast with the equivalent list of immediate left collocates of *that* in Conversational Production is dramatic (Table 11).

As we are mainly dealing with determiners rather than subordinators when we look at *that* in Conversational Production, it is not surprising that *and* – number two in both lists – arises in contrasting grammatical contexts when

Table 9. Left collocates of that in Written Academic – frequency

so	suggest	believe	showed
and	means	follows	shown
is	was	out	those
fact	note	than	true
in	with	be	as
argued	say	but	assuming
clear	said	concluded	claim
suggested	to	establishes	for
of	reveals	estimated	
notice	show	idea	
such	evidence	seen	
suggests	belief	think	
found	believed	or	
shows	ensure	provided	

Table 10. Verbs

ARGUE	ASSUME	BELIEVE	CLAIM
CONCLUDE	ENSURE	ESTABLISH	ESTIMATE
FIND	MEAN	NOTE	NOTICE
REVEAL	SAY	SEE	SHOW
SUGGEST	THINK		

Table 11. Left collocates of "that" in Conversational Production

like	that	mean	cos
and	for	it	that's
yeah	not	think	had
well	no	say	you
is	about	see	did
so	at	was	than
do	what's	get	there
all	but	got	be
of	on	if	up
know	one	said	want
oh	have	to	words
in	with	put	yes
		right	does

compared with *and that* in Written Academic. Thus, there are only four instances of *and that is* in Written Academic, whereas there are 51 in Conversational Production (out of a total of 146), and Written Academic contains none

of the *all that, know that, what's that* or *that's that* forms which figure so largely in Conversational Production.

Looking at a middle ground: Keywords in Fiction and Spoken Academic

If we were able to use KW analysis to typify core aspects of the strongly contrasting discourses of Written Academic and Conversational Production, what of the hybrids Fiction and Spoken Academic?

Spoken Academic and Fiction Keywords referenced against BNC Sampler Written

As with the earlier analysis, two keyword lists have been generated for each set of files, one referenced against BNC Sampler Written (see Table 12 for the top 20), the other against BNC Sampler Spoken (see Table 13 for this top 20).

Table 12. Content and function keywords in Spoken Academic and Fiction (referenced against BNCW)

N	Spoken Academic_BNCW Content	Function	Freq.	Fiction_BNCW Content	Function	Freq.
1		ERM	228	MASKLIN		515
2		ER	205	ANGALO		298
3		THAT	817	GURDER		275
4	CHANNELS		110	SAID		860
5		SO	309		I	1,447
6		WE	404	THING		345
7	MILL		64		N'T	689
8	CALCIUM		53		IT	1,377
9	MEMBRANE		48	NOMES		139
10		VE	114		YOU	902
11		ED	57	HUMANS		153
12		YOU	404		D	234
13		VERY	181	SHIP		105
14		OKAY	54		HE	802
15	CHANNEL		87		DO	411
16		IT	605	NOME		68
17	ACTUALLY		69		S	923
18		THIS	396		VE	150
19	DEMOCRACY		58	KNOW		207
20		HERE	124		RE	195

Table 13. Content and function keywords in Spoken Academic and Fiction (referenced against BNCS)

N	Spoken Academic_BNCS Content	Function	Freq.	Fiction_BNCS Content	Function	Freq.
1	CHANNELS		110	MASKLIN		515
2		OF	1,245	ANGALO		298
3	CHANNEL		87	GURDER		275
4	MILL		64	SAID		860
5	CALCIUM		53	HUMANS		153
6	DEMOCRACY		58	NOMES		139
7	MEMBRANE		48	SHIP		105
8		WHICH	277	THING		345
9	POTASSIUM		34	NOME		68
10	RUSSELL		49	HUMAN		82
11	VOTE		53	LOOKED		125
12	TUPLE		30	GRANDSON		54
13	GATED		27	STORE		66
14	HUMAN		41	PION		43
15		IS	642	FROGS		40
16	VOLTAGE		28		HIS	249
17		THE	1,934	ISABEL		31
18	ACTIVATED		23	SKY		45
19	PATTERN		30	GEESE		33
20	STIMULUS		21		TAE	29

Looking first at function words, we see that the top 20 keyword lists for Spoken Academic and Fiction referenced against BNCW give an immediate sense of the words that are required for the elaboration of the vocal and inter-active aspects of the texts. In Spoken Academic the dialogic (but asymmetric) nature of the lecture is signalled by the transcript equivalents of hesitation signals and the dominant personal pronouns *we* and *you* (note – *not* I). The third person singular form of the verb *to be* is also exceptionally prominent – and a quick review of immediate left collocates shows us that *is* is typically associated with *this / which / it / that / there / do / what* – most of which are anaphoric cohesive devices and / or involved in clause elaboration. Importantly, although Spoken Academic is the transcript of *spoken* production, it appears to share characteristics with written production, thus *that* is mainly a subordinating conjunction (CJT = 445 / DT0 = 337). The function of *very, okay* and *here* are also important, as they show the lecturers' tendency to evaluate (VERY), signal shifts in the direction of the argument – closing one passage and opening another (OK) and the need to address phenomena outside the text (usually on display panels, diagrams or models).

So far as content is concerned (*channels / mill / calcium / membrane / channel / actually / democracy*), we get an immediate impression of the content focus of the more specialist lecture transcripts,[5] and that at least one of the texts in Fiction is dealing with some fairly weird phenomena (*Masklin, Angalo, Gurder, Nome* – all of which come from the BNC file CEU – the Terry Pratchett novel).

Spoken Academic and Fiction Keywords referenced against BNC Spoken

The keywords for Spoken Academic and Fiction tell a related but very differently nuanced story.

While many of the same content keywords are present, the pattern of function words represented stands in marked contrast to the BNCW referenced set. Of first importance is the presence of *of* and *the* as keywords in Spoken Academic. While none of us may want to speak like a book, the lecturers and presenters in this set, seem to be moving in that direction when they are compared with other speakers. Similarly, their tendency to position their discourse in a timeless present is marked, along with their need to qualify or refer to previous text elements through the use of relative clauses. In Fiction, it begins to be possible to get a clearer sense of the protagonists and focus of the two novels in the set. While the majority of the items come from CEU (the Pratchett novel), at least we learn that *Isabel* is the central character of B38 (the Lockhead contribution to BNC). We are also now able to see that CEU (178 of the 249 instances of he) is a third person narrative, with mainly male characters, whereas B38 has 139 of the 197 instances of *she* (Keyword rank 271) and 136 of the 165 instances of *her* (Keyword rank 216).

Perhaps more importantly, and a final comment in this chapter, there is the information we get from *negative* keywords. Scott comments that: "A word which is negatively key occurs less often than would be expected by chance in comparison with the reference corpus" (1999). The five most negative keywords for Spoken Academic (referenced against BNC Sampler Spoken) are: *no / know / oh / you / I*. The lecturers in this set tend neither to be negative, claim either that they or other people know things, use exclamations, or use "I" as much as people do in the reference corpus, or say *you* and *I* as much as a larger population. In Fiction referenced against BNC Sampler Spoken , we find. *I / oh / you / that / yeah / er* as negative keywords. These two texts would not appear to be first person narratives (or there's little dialogue with first person engagement) and the speech style of the characters seems to be a little more formal and decisive than that of real speakers.

Conclusions

We set out in this chapter to consider the extent to which KW analysis might be useful in profiling four sets of texts and to see if pedagogically useful conclusions could be arrived at on the basis of this analysis. We feel that that the journey has been worthwhile and that KW analysis offers a surprisingly effective way building an understanding of what's going on in a text. However, we should add that this understanding comes not from the most obvious results found on the keyword list, but often comes in from left-field as a result of looking at the function words that float to the surface as a result of statistical processing.

What this chapter has shown in particular is that it is possible to give students rapid access to key information about texts which might interest them (for example, the verb list in Table 10 – Verbs). Depending on the texts selected, teachers could use the results of such analysis in the elaboration of language awareness-awareness raising courses at the beginning of programmes, and, working with more advanced learners, as a means of helping writers or speakers to extend their productive range in genres or discourse areas relevant to their interests and needs.

Notes

1. The examples used here are from the BNC, but the approach could be applied to any text collections which a teacher has access to and which are appropriate for their learners.

2. POS = part of speech. In the BNC every word has been allocated a part of speech label called a "tag".

3. Collocates are taken as being any co-occurring words across a pre-determined left/right span. Immediate collocates are those words directly before or after the node word in a concordance.

4. Adam Kilgariif's wordlists – http://www.itri.bton.ac.uk/~Adam.Kilgarriff/ (reference 1-Apr-03).

5. Two lectures, in fact: MILL is John Stuart, and linked with DEMOCRACY in HUF, the political philosophy lecture, and CHANNEL, CALCIUM and MEMBRANE come from J86, bioenergetics.

## CHAPTER 7

Business and professional communication
Managing relationships in professional writing

Summary

In this chapter we show how KW analysis can be used to identify words that are important in discourse moves critical to the management of writer/reader relationships in professional correspondence. We then go on to develop a more finely nuanced account of such relationships through a close examination of variations in the linguistic contexts in which these words are used. A combination of KW analysis and discourse analysis offers teachers and students a powerful way of coming to an understanding of how language is used in professional settings.

Introduction

Nelson 2000 reports that "Business English appears similar to general English, with only a small amount of business lexis appearing amongst the most frequent words" (Nelson 2000: Ch. 10.1). Although he goes on to report the significant contrasts that exist between the business and non-business collocations, colligations and semantic prosodies (cf. Louw 1993; Hoey 1997) of the frequent words in his Business English corpus, the fact remains that the actual lexis of business and professional communication does not differ greatly from the lexis of written communication in general.

While the words used in business and professional writing may be largely the same as those used in any other written communication, we agree with Nelson that the professional writer will tend to use these words in different ways when compared with other writers. We also predict that there will be further variation when the different roles that writers take on when constructing relationships with a range of readers are taken into account. In this chapter, we will consider ways in which keywords in business and professional communication texts – and the contrasting collocations, colligations and semantic prosodies of these keywords – can give insights into how writers use language to build and maintain relationships within and outside an organisation.

Resources

The data we will use is part of a small personal corpus of professional correspondence (letters and faxes) which was compiled between 1992–1994 (before email became widely used in British organisations). During this period, one of the authors was responsible for the management of UK supported social development projects in countries which had recently emerged from incorporation in the Soviet Union. The collection consists of correspondence between two individual managers and their colleagues, clients and professional partners (along with a small number of personal communications to friends and family members). One collection (BUSL1) comprises 679 items, the other (BUSL2) 348 items.[1] The majority of the texts in the collection can be classed as "letters". A small number can be classed as "faxes". Unfortunately, memos from the period were not retained.

Approach

A starting assumption for this study has been that this kind of correspondence can be categorised on the basis of where it is positioned in relation to four cardinal points: INTERNAL or EXTERNAL, CLOSE or DISTANT. We have found this categorisation to be robust and illuminating when considering correspondence. Within this framework, a text can be allocated to a position in one of four quadrants. The example diagram below (Figure 1) show three hypothetical texts which are similar in their external/internal positioning, but which are progressively more distant along the close/distant axes.

In order to enrich subsequent analyses a manual analysis of all the texts in the correspondence collections was undertaken. This involved the tagging of each text in the collection to enable review of five text categories (Table 1).

There were no instances of INT_PERS (Internal Personal texts). All instances of EXT_PERS were of correspondence with family members or friends being written to for non-professional reasons. They cannot be mapped directly in this model, but we predict that they share many features of texts at the extreme of the INT_CLOSE category.

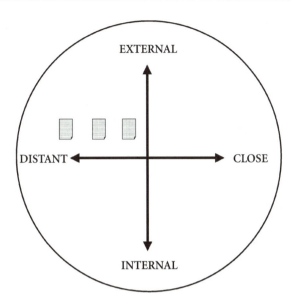

Figure 1. Text map

Allocation of texts in BUSL1 and BUSL2 to internal/external categories was established on the basis of the recipient address of the correspondent (external correspondents do not work within the organisation, internal correspondents work either in closely associated offices or within the broader organisation). Members of the close/distant category were identified on the basis of privileged insider knowledge. If we a) knew the recipient of a text well and b) the communicative purpose of the text was not face threatening, the text was tagged *close*. If the recipient was either little known, and/or the correspondence was potentially face threatening, the text was tagged *distant*. The categories and map will form an integral part of the analysis that is developed in the rest of this chapter.

Table 1. Text categories in the collection

TAG	MEANING	BUSL1	BUSL2
<EXT_CLOSE>	External close	3	28
<EXT_DIST>	External distant	668	284
<EXT_PERS>	External personal	3	23
<INT_CLOSE>	Internal close	0	8
<INT_DIST>	Internal distant	5	5
	TOTALS	679	348

In the rest of this chapter we will outline and apply a research methodology which, we feel, can be deployed in a broad range of pedagogically oriented contexts. The methodology involves the identification of a keyword or set of keywords which are likely to give insights into how writers work in specific genres, and the systematic analysis of the collocational, colligational, and discoursal relationships that keywords enter into. In this present instance, we will only deal with one keyword. The keyword list for the text collection we studied offered another 343 possible starting points: quite a rich resource.

Preliminary analysis

This investigation started from a review of a keyword list for the smaller text collection BUSL2.[2] In this list, the first full verb form is "hope"[3] (following "will", "am", "I'm", and "it's"). This keyword was chosen as the focus for the study to be outlined in this chapter, both for its prominence in this corpus and also because we were aware of its potential importance in the construction of writer/reader interactions. The choice was fortunate as it took us almost directly to four texts (Figures 2–5) which provide a useful starting point for a discussion of writer/reader relationships. In this section of the chapter we will briefly comment on each text and present an analysis of its social function, along with the moves required to realise this function.

The move categories used here draw on earlier work by Sinclair and Coulthard (1975) and the approach outlined in practical applications such as that of Swales (1981) and Dudley-Evans (1994). Most of the categories have been given names which we consider to be reasonably transparent. The Situation Problem Result Evaluation – SPRE – minimal discourse pattern (Winter 1977; Hoey 1983; Hoey & Winter 1986) is also used as a means of extending this move analysis. Purely conventional elements like Header, Salutation and Closure are not included in the overall move analysis, although they are marked. In the present instance we feel that *statement of context, rejection, request for action*, and so forth do not need further explanation. *Channel maintainer*, however, may be less obvious. We see this as an important move in the correspondence of client oriented service organisations as it signals that writer wishes to continue to maintain a relationship with the reader, whatever the outcomes of the earlier moves in the letter.

Example A

Example A is written to an *external* reader and has the major communicative purpose of *rejecting*. We categorised it as EXT_DIST. The text has three major moves (one of which extends from the second sentence (break marked thus ||) through to the sentence preceding the closure

1. Statement of context
2. Rejection
3. Channel maintainer

Header	DATE
	ADDRESS
	–
Salutation	Dear PROPER_NAME,
1/ statement of context	Thank you for your letter of DATE in which you asked for an application form for the Trainer Training programme.
2/ rejection 3/ channel maintainer ↓ ↓ ↓ ↓	I am afraid that you were too late to be considered for this programme and that another teacher from the PROPER_NAME region has been asked to take on this responsibility. || I would, however, very much like to thank you for your interest in the course and **hope** that you will be able to cooperate with the new trainer when she starts her work in PROPER_NAME in January of DATE.
Closure	My best wishes for the rest of the summer,
	Yours sincerely, PROPER_NAME, JOB_TITLE

Figure 2. Example A

Example B

This short note is more complex: an *apology* which is not an apology? On the basis of insider knowledge, We categorised the text as EXT_CLOSE. Although it is written to a manager in an external organisation, the text forms part of an extensive correspondence and there is an implicit equality in the power relationship. The message is complex, with some form of apology or a justification implicit in the text, but no specific performative speech act or similar lexical signal being used. The complexity of the message is compounded by having

Header	DATE
	ADDRESS
	–
Salutation	Dear PROPER_NAME,
1/ situation	I enclose pink forms + registers for the PROPER_NAME tests held at the
2/ problem	PROPER_NAME Centre on DATE; DATE; DATE. ‖ I have a problem with
3/ response	the pink form for PROPER_NAME – I can't trace it. ‖ I have issued the
4/ channel	certificate and enclose a photocopy of my yellow form. ‖ – I __hope__ this is not
maintainer	the end of the world - I could always have typed out another form and
	thrown away the bits I didn't need, I suppose …
Closure	
	Best regards,
	PROPER_NAME, JOB_TITLE

Figure 3. Example B

four separate moves within a single paragraph (boundaries are again marked thus: ‖).

An adapted Situation, Problem, Response, Evaluation (SPRE) minimal discourse pattern provides a basis for resolving some of the interpretational problems. Thus a possible analysis of the moves is:

1.   Statement of situation
2.   Statement of problem
3.   Statement of response
4.   Channel maintainer

A similar simplified Problem / Solution model would also have explanatory force for Example A, in that the Move 2 (rejection) can be seen as constituting the Problem element with Move 3 (channel maintainer) as a solution – come on chaps, let's be civilised… Move 4 in B4 appears to operate in the same way.

Example C

This letter is also an example of communication with an external reader, but here the writer is providing a valued service and is in a position to request action from the reader – the power relationship is slightly weighted in the writer's favour. The main communicative purpose of the letter is, therefore, *request for action*, the category in our analysis is again EXT_DIST. The moves can be characterised as follows:

Header	DATE
	ADDRESS
Salutation	–
	Dear PROPER_NAME,
1/ context	I am pleased to be able to enclose the master tapes for PROPER_NAME –
2/ request	the course for teachers of English. ‖ This is the only set of masters which
	exists in PROPER_NAME and I would, therefore, be grateful if you could
3/ justification	return them to us (via PROPER_NAME) once you have finished your
	broadcasts. ‖ It is possible that other radio stations will be interested in
	broadcasting them in the future, and I will need to pass over the masters to
	these other companies.
4/ channel	
maintainer	I **hope** that the programmes are successful – please do keep me up-to-date
	on any reactions you get from your listeners.
Closure	
	Best wishes,
	PROPER_NAME, JOB_TITLE

Figure 4. Example C

1. Statement of context
2. Request for action
3. Justification for request
4. Channel maintainer

Example D

The final example is also a *request for action*, but arises from a different communicative context as it is from one colleague to another (INT_CLOSE). Although there an asymmetric power relationship – the writer is the line manager of the reader – there is, nevertheless, a degree of intimacy in the communication which is lacking from the three previous examples. The fax has three moves with the following functions:

1. Statement of context
2. Request for action
3. Channel maintainer

Fax header	FROM:	PROPER_NAME, JOB_TITLE
	TO:	PROPER_NAME, JOB_TITLE
	FAX:	NUMBER
	PAGES	1
	DATE:	DATE
	SUBJECT:	Management meeting

	PROPER_NAME –
Salutation	
	Home safe and sound!
1/ context	I attach a copy of my notes from today's meeting. Can you check if I've got it
2/ request	right and get back to me if I've missed anything?
3/ channel maintainer	I may not see you until later in DATE as I'm off to PROPER_NAME next week and then on Holiday from the 3rd. I **hope** that the event in PROPER_NAME goes well – sorry I'm missing it. I look forward to seeing the suit!
Closure	
	Best regards
	PROPER_NAME, JOB_TITLE

Figure 5. Example D

Preliminary analysis: Discussion

A reading of these four examples – originally chosen because they all contained the word *hope* – offers an insight into the range of roles the writer of BUSL2 takes on. A possible mapping is given below in Figure 6.

We were interested to find such a wide range of distribution, given that the texts were all written within the constraints of one bureaucratic organisation and by the same author. A second, and more significant finding is that although the four examples are distributed in different sectors of our map, the keyword *hope* occurs in the same moves in all four examples – *channel maintainer*. This unpredicted observation raises the possibility that we can use specific lexical items to spot different moves in a collection of texts written within the same organisation or analogues of that organisation. This would have pedagogic potential as it would not only indicate moves that are likely to be required but also ways of realising these moves. It would point to another possible insight into language use in professional settings. If different mappings are associated with systematic contrasts in the colligations and collocations of the keywords, there may be the possibility of helping apprentice writers gain fuller control of the genres they are learning to work with.

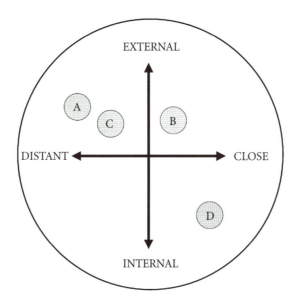

Figure 6. Text mapping 1

Our four examples already indicate that this might be the case. Thus, in Example B (Close/External) and Example D (Close/Internal), *hope* is found in the following sentence contexts:

B. I **hope** this is not the end of the world – I could always have typed out another form and thrown away the bits I didn't need, I suppose ....
D. I **hope** that the event in PROPER_NAME goes well – sorry I'm missing it.

... whereas *hope* occurs in the following sentence contexts in Examples A, and C (Distant/External):

A. I would, however, very much like to thank you for your interest in the course and **hope** that you will be able to cooperate with the new trainer when she starts her work in PROPER_NAME in January of DATE.
C. I **hope** that the programmes are successful – please do keep me up-to-date on any reactions you get from your listeners

Major contrasts between the pairs B/D and A/C are that in the former we find evidence of:

–   contracted forms (*didn't, I'm*)

- ellipsis – conjunction *that* in B and D / personal pronoun *I* in D.
- vague language (*bits*)

… while in the latter, these features either do not occur or occur with lower frequency or intensity. Such formal contrasts are consistent with the views of Biber (1988) and Halliday (1989) in their accounts of the differences between spoken and written production.

These formal contrasts are situated in another kind of difference: the contrasting lexical densities of the two opposed samples. Halliday (1989) considers lexical density to be an important component in the structure of formal written production when compared with informal conversational production. An example of this contrast is given in the analysis below (following Halliday 1989) where the ratio of clauses to lexical is calculated. In this instance:

- *lexical* words contrast with *grammar* or function words which have no independent meaning, and
- a clause is either main, coordinated or subordinate (including those clauses where there is ellipsis of discoursally redundant elements).

In the analysis below clause boundaries are indicated by numbers between vertical bars (e.g. |1|). Lexical items are numbered in bold italics and underlined (e.g. *1* <u>word</u>). The lexical density is establish by a simple division of the number of lexical items in the text by the total number of clauses.

> Example A
> |1| I would, however, very much *1* <u>like</u> to *2* <u>thank</u> you for your *3* <u>interest</u> in the *4* <u>course</u> |2| and *5* <u>hope</u> that you will be *6* <u>able</u> to *7* <u>cooperate</u> with the *8* <u>new</u> *9* <u>trainer</u> |3| when she *10* <u>starts</u> her *11* <u>work</u> in *12* <u>PROPER_NAME</u> in *13* <u>January</u> of *14* <u>DATE</u>.

Lexical density index: 14:3 = 4.6

> Example B
> |1| I *1* <u>hope</u> |2| this is not the *2* <u>end</u> of the *3* <u>world</u> |3| – I *4* <u>could</u> always have *5* <u>typed</u> out another *6* <u>form</u> and |4| *7* <u>thrown</u> away the *8* <u>bits</u> |5| I didn't *9* <u>need</u>, |6| I *10* <u>suppose</u>

Lexical density index 10:6 = 1.6

A comparatively high lexical density such as that of Example A is typical of formal written production. The lower lexical density of B is much closer to the structure of spoken conversation. Relative lexical density can be used as a further means of distinguishing between close and distant texts.

In the next section of this chapter we will look at the extent to which such contrasts in the colligations, collocations, discourse environments, and lexico-grammatical environments of keywords in BUSL2 can be used to predict the mapping of individual texts on the matrix given above. Our working hypothesis is that if the keyword *hope* in bureaucratic correspondence occurs in the contexts outlined above, the writers of these texts are engaged in more or less distant relationships with their correspondents. If it *is* possible to use keywords as tracers not only of the aboutness of a text (Scott 1997a), but also of the relationship between writer and reader (and this chapter is written in an exploratory and experimental spirit in which we are testing potential rather than comfortably reporting established conclusions!) then it begins to be possible to argue even more strongly for the value of KW analysis in the specification of genres.

KW analysis – *hope*

Discourse moves

We mentioned above that *hope* occurred in a move we called *channel maintainer* and that this move occurred as a final stage in the development of the texts. Before considering the linguistic contexts in which *hope* occurs in BUSL2 we will review its positioning across the texts in the collection. This can be done using the "plot" feature in Wordsmith Tools Concord program. Results are summarised in the chart in Figure 7.

The implications of this initial analysis is that the great majority of instances of *hope* that we are considering in the sections which follow are located in equivalent discourse moves and are, therefore, implicated in the same discourse functions. We will now review three aspects of the environments in which *hope* occurs: contractions, ellipsis, vague language + informal idioms, and lexical density.

Contractions

Using the keyword list for BUSL2 (referenced against a BNC Sampler Written wordlist), as a starting point, the following contractions list (Table 2) has been developed.

As a simple first test of the writer/reader relationship in *channel maintaining* moves, we traced all instances of *hope* which occur in the same environment

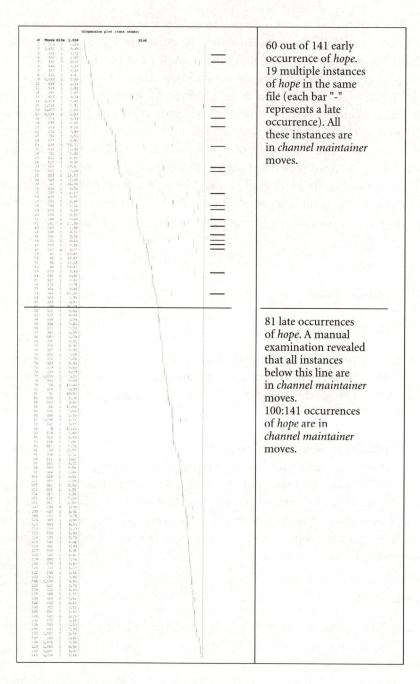

Figure 7. Position of "hope" in correspondence text

Table 2. Contractions

CAN'T	HE'S	SHE'S	I'RE
DIDN'T	I'D	THERE'S	I'VE
DON'T	I'LL	THEY'RE	WON'T
HADN'T	I'M IT'S	I'D	YOU'RE
HAVEN'T	I'VE	I'LL	

as these contractions. For this search a freeware Windows program WAny-Word (http://home4.inet.tele.dk/jensguld/) was used. As this allows Boolean searching across text files it was simple to search for *hope plus* a list of these contractions or *excluding* them. The following results were obtained:

	EXT_DIST	EXT_CLOSE	EXT_PERS	INT_CLOSE	INT_DIST
hope-contractions					
98 out of 348 texts	96	2	0	0	0
hope+contractions					
48 out of 348 texts	17	14	15	2	0

A manual review of the 98 hope -contractions texts

EXTERNAL/DISTANT immediately indicated in the majority of cases the recipient is one of these:

- client
- service provider
- partner

In only 16 cases where the letter EXTERNAL/CLOSE the recipients are known to the author but are being thanked for services or support that have been provided professionally.

A review of the 48 texts in which *hope* +contractions occurs shows that they are less consistently situated in one area of the map. These results can be mapped as in Figure 8.

The absence of texts in the INTERNAL hemisphere is no surprise given the small numbers of such texts in the collection as a whole. It was, however, interesting to note that there were no instances if INT_DIST texts containing the term *hope* – an indication of a lack of desire to maintain open channels in such circumstances? Although not surprising, the very strong correlation between the absence of contractions and the mapping of texts to the DISTANT quadrant should be noted. Given that all the PERSONAL communications and CLOSE communications contain contractions, it is likely that communications which

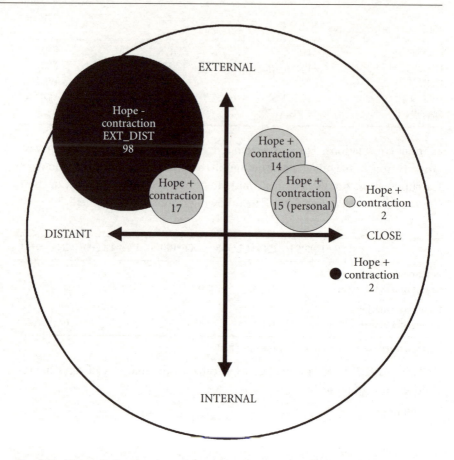

Figure 8. Text mapping 2

we have classed as distant and which contain contraction form an intermediate case where there is a movement towards a *closer* style.

Ellipsis

We noted in the initial analysis that *hope* + ellipsis appeared to be a second feature of *close* texts. This pattern is relatively easy to identify in texts by using the context word feature in WordSmith (hope in the context of *not* that) – or simply by re-sorting a concordance. We considered all instances where *hope* was followed by a pronoun or an article to be instances of ellipsis. *Hope to* was not treated as ellipsis.

Table 3. Ellipsis + "that"

	Total	+that	–that	+to
<EXT_CLOSE>	19	10	9	1
<EXT_DIST>	123	70	53	11
<EXT_PERS>	25	5	20	0
<INT_CLOSE>	2	2	0	0
<INT_DIST>	0	0	0	0
	181	87	82	12

Table 4. Hope –that

Word	R1
YOU	19
THIS	14
THE	9
IT	7
FOR	3
NOT	2
THERE	2
WILL	2
A	1

The overall distribution of hope +/– ellipsis of *that* is summarised in Table 3.

From this data there is some evidence that writers prefer to use full forms in EXT_DIST texts (70:53), and vice-versa in EXT_PERS, the most intimate of the texts in the collection (20:5). EXT_CLOSE texts appear to be an interesting middle ground with an even split. If *hope + non-finite verb* is included with hope + *conjunction that* as a distancing form, then the count of that + *distancer* in EXT_DIST becomes 81, with no instances of *hope + non-finite verb* in INT_CLOSE or EXT_PERS.

In the instances where there was ellipsis of *that* the following words occurred in the immediate right context of **hope** (Table 4).

Interestingly, the most frequent **hope –that** forms (hope + *you*, hope + *this*, hope + *the*) occur with the similar ranked frequency to their **hope +that** equivalents, indicating that the decision to use ellipsis is not imposed because the word is being used in strikingly different verbal contexts.

Table 5. Hope +that

Word	R2
YOU	23
THE	17
THIS	16
I	6
YOUR	6
IT	4
THESE	3
I	1

Table 6. Vague language

	Total files	+vague
<EXT_CLOSE>	28	24
<EXT_DIST>	284	150
<EXT_PERS>	23	21
<INT_CLOSE>	8	5
<INT_DIST>	5	4
	348	204

Vague language

While vague language is impossible to track automatically, it is a relatively straightforward process to identify a small set of vague words and idioms using the keyword tool. In the first instance a reference corpus of academic texts in the BNC was made to generate a reference wordlist. This selection was chosen as it was the one least likely to contain large amounts of this kind of lexis. A vague language oriented keyword list for BUS1 is given below:

get/feel/got/lot/bit

There were 394 instances of these words in a total of 204 files. Distribution across the corpus was as in Table 6.

Results for this analysis are suggestive as almost all the EXT_CLOSE, INT_CLOSE and EXT_PERS files contain vague language as compared with just over 50% of the EXT_DIST set. The vague language instances in INT_DIST were all "get" and seem to have been used in contexts where the writer is either involved in a request for action (and reducing face threat through the use of an idiom (1,3,4) or apologising and using an idiom in an attempt to diminish the writer's culpability for a delay in acting (5). The instance that does not seem to

```
1.     you are able, it will help me  get my house in order at this en
2.  ow later in the week, he should  get a good sense of the wintry s
3.    for getting there. If you can  get back to me on this as soon a
4.              b. check on price c.  get back to me as soon as possib
5.    e! Sorry for the delay, but it  got to the back of a pile! I ha
```

Figure 9. "Get" in informal correspondence

E.g. 1.   <EXT_DIST>
           |i) I would also 1 hope |ii| that you could then 2   14 lexical items
           participate with 3 <proper_noun>, 4 Head of the 5   2 clauses
           Department of 6 <proper_noun>at 7   *Lexical density 7*
           <proper_noun>University, 8 <proper_noun> from 9
           <proper_noun> 10 <proper_noun> 11 University and
           12 <proper_noun>, in a 13 panel 14 discussion.

E.g. 2.   <EXT_PERS>
           |i| I *1* hope |ii| *2* all is *3* well with you *4* all.   4lexical items
                                                                        2 clauses
                                                                        Lexical density 2

Figure 10. Lexical density

fit any pattern is (2) – part of a consistently informal correspondence between the manager and an external professional contact.

Lexical density

A manual review of the sentence contexts in which *hope* is used in BUSL2 indicates a contrast between the lexical density of the contexts in the major text category (EXT_DIST> and the closer categories (EXT_CLOSE, EXT_PERS and INT_CLOSE). This contrast is not absolute at a sentence level – and we did not expect this to be the case – but it does range from extreme examples such as 1 with a lexical density of 7, down to Example 2 with a lexical density of 2. We have not undertaken an exhaustive study of this aspect of the texts, but certainly found that the EXT_DIST set has more instances of high lexical density than did *close* texts such as EXT_PERS.

KW analysis: Discussion

From the starting point of a single keyword, it has been possible to test the working hypothesis in Analysis 1. A summary of the results of the analysis might be the following advice to apprentice writers:

> When writing to close contacts and colleagues, our example writer felt free to use contractions, ellipsis and vague language. When writing to external contacts and in potentially face threatening contexts, the writer tended to avoid these linguistic features.

While this advice may not be strikingly original, it is advice based on evidence rather than intuition, and that evidence constitutes a pedagogic resource that the learner can use as a scaffold around which they can construct their own, independent performances. In the next chapter we will extend this discussion of writing in professional contexts to review the construction of arguments and relationships in academic writing.

Notes

1. The text collection has been anonymised for research purposes but cannot be put in the public domain for reasons of confidentiality.

2. See the Appendix for the top 100 keywords for BUSL2.

3. When the concordance for *hope* in L1 was checked it was found that all 200 instances are verbs.

Appendix

BUSL2 – Keyword list (Proper Nouns replaced throughout)

Key word	Freq.	%	RC. Freq.	RC. %	Keyness
LANGUAGE	620	0.55	98	0.01	2,404.79
PROPER_NOUN	709	0.63	250	0.02	2,330.99
PROPER_NOUN	643	0.57	227	0.02	2,113.00
PROPER_NOUN	434	0.39	27	0.00	1,869.69
TEACHING	439	0.39	48	0.00	1,789.68
PROPER_NOUN	705	0.63	650	0.06	1,613.19
TRIBBLE	321	0.29	0	0.00	1,530.82
CONSULTANT	342	0.30	16	0.00	1,503.38
YOU	1,587	1.41	4,469	0.40	1,472.99
I	2,039	1.82	7,126	0.64	1,396.80
PROPER_NOUN	310	0.28	10	0.00	1,391.26
PROPER_NOUN	282	0.25	9	0.00	1,266.19
DEAR	347	0.31	85	0.01	1,242.85
PROPER_NOUN	265	0.24	2	0.00	1,240.46
STATES	390	0.35	184	0.02	1,175.47
PROPER_NOUN	224	0.20	10	0.00	987.37
TEACHERS	241	0.21	40	0.00	926.90
PROPER_NOUN	188	0.17	2	0.00	874.54
SINCERELY	169	0.15	5	0.00	761.35
#	5,223	4.65	33,835	3.06	740.06
YOUR	666	0.59	1,605	0.15	739.00
ABLE	300	0.27	239	0.02	736.48
ELT	178	0.16	22	0.00	714.30
YOURS	185	0.16	35	0.00	696.02
TRAINING	258	0.23	169	0.02	689.63
WILL	932	0.83	3,143	0.28	671.33
AM	310	0.28	330	0.03	655.45
CONFERENCE	217	0.19	115	0.01	628.49
PROGRAMME	252	0.22	202	0.02	616.79
I'M	127	0.11	0	0.00	605.45
Œ	126	0.11	0	0.00	600.68
PROPER_NOUN	107	0.10	0	0.00	510.09
IT'S	106	0.09	0	0.00	505.32
PROPER_NOUN	101	0.09	0	0.00	481.48
HOPE	200	0.18	166	0.02	481.45
PROPER_NOUN	122	0.11	19	0.00	473.80
PROPER_NOUN	106	0.09	4	0.00	471.73
PROPER_NOUN	97	0.09	0	0.00	462.41

Key word	Freq.	%	RC. Freq.	RC. %	Keyness
PROPER_NOUN	100	0.09	3	0.00	450.16
PROJECT	232	0.21	286	0.03	449.02
BE	1,392	1.24	7,098	0.64	436.44
BEST	251	0.22	369	0.03	431.24
I	830	0.74	3,421	0.31	422.39
MS	124	0.11	40	0.00	416.67
UNIVERSITY	303	0.27	590	0.05	414.82
WISHES	113	0.10	31	0.00	394.68
PROPER_NOUN	120	0.11	46	0.00	385.02
FORWARD	157	0.14	126	0.01	383.95
GRATEFUL	104	0.09	23	0.00	380.07
FOR	1,778	1.58	10,451	0.95	360.84
LETTER	157	0.14	148	0.01	354.57
EDUCATION	164	0.15	171	0.02	350.69
PROVIDE	194	0.17	266	0.02	350.00
THANKS	118	0.11	64	0.01	338.87
PLEASED	113	0.10	55	0.00	336.88
DIRECTOR	147	0.13	148	0.01	320.49
ENCLOSE	70	0.06	2	0.00	315.79
PROPER_NOUN	73	0.06	5	0.00	311.81
SUE	74	0.07	8	0.00	301.87
WOULD	598	0.53	2,475	0.22	301.48
VERY	362	0.32	1,134	0.10	289.81
REGARDS	71	0.06	11	0.00	275.93
WRITING	119	0.11	115	0.01	265.22
TEACHER	101	0.09	69	0.01	265.22
DON'T	54	0.05	0	0.00	257.40
PEDAGOGICAL	53	0.05	0	0.00	252.64
TOPIC	73	0.06	24	0.00	244.09
THANK	117	0.10	129	0.01	242.28
DEVELOPMENT	166	0.15	304	0.03	239.77
CC	55	0.05	3	0.00	239.14
PROPER_NOUN	50	0.04	0	0.00	238.34
CHEQUE	56	0.05	4	0.00	238.32
TRAINERS	60	0.05	8	0.00	238.29
SUPPORT	167	0.15	314	0.03	235.75
MINISTRY	86	0.08	56	0.01	230.33
PROPER_NOUN	47	0.04	0	0.00	224.03
PROPER_NOUN	165	0.15	325	0.03	223.43
PROPER_NOUN	46	0.04	0	0.00	219.27
FAX	57	0.05	10	0.00	217.17
THIS	867	0.77	4,777	0.43	216.62
IATEFL	45	0.04	0	0.00	214.50

Key word	Freq.	%	RC. Freq.	RC. %	Keyness
IF	490	0.44	2,184	0.20	211.73
SCHOOL	155	0.14	307	0.03	208.82
PROFESSIONAL	92	0.08	90	0.01	203.70
I'VE	41	0.04	0	0.00	195.43
SYLLABUS	42	0.04	1	0.00	190.89
JUNE	99	0.09	128	0.01	185.73
PROPER_NOUN	61	0.05	28	0.00	185.35
PROPER_NOUN	38	0.03	0	0.00	181.13
I'RE	38	0.03	0	0.00	181.13
CONTACT	99	0.09	133	0.01	181.05
PROPER_NOUN	42	0.04	4	0.00	173.79
THINGS	138	0.12	297	0.03	171.79
PROPER_NOUN	36	0.03	0	0.00	171.60
I'VE	36	0.03	0	0.00	171.60
TH	130	0.12	270	0.02	167.51
UNIT	80	0.07	87	0.01	166.97
REGARDING	54	0.05	24	0.00	165.76
PROPER_NOUN	34	0.03	0	0.00	162.06
CONSULTANCY	42	0.04	7	0.00	161.36

## CHAPTER 8

English for academic purposes

Building an account of expert and apprentice performances in literary criticism

Summary

In this chapter we show how corpus phenomena which Scott (1997) calls *clusters* can be used to investigate contrast between expert and apprentice production in an area of academic writing. Working with a collection of Polish literature MA student dissertations and published literary criticism articles from the BNC, we demonstrate how clusters can be used to identify pedagogically useful contrasts between these text collections.

Introduction

This chapter focuses on insights we can gain through the analysis of what Scott calls *clusters*: i.e. groups of "words which follow each other in a text" (Scott 1997a). Clusters are fundamentally the same as what Biber et al. (2000) call lexical bundles. While they may have some overlap with categories such as collocations or idioms (Sinclair 1991), or prefabs (Cowie 2001), what is important in the context of corpus analysis using Wordsmith Tools is that clusters begin life as purely distributional phenomena. Thus, if a particular (2, 3, 4 etc.) combination of words is identified as occurring above a specific frequency limit (e.g. 5) within a research text or text collection, this combination is a "cluster". For lexical bundles, Biber et al. decided on a limit of 20 instances per million words when dealing with a large corpus (Biber et al. 2000:990) and we have followed this practice. Clusters unlike keywords are not arrived at through a statistical comparison of one collection of texts with a reference corpus. However, they offer an alternative means of differentiating between texts in different corpora.

Table 1. 3 word clusters in BNC_ALL

N	BNC_ALL	Freq.	Norm.
1	one of the	35,603	360
2	the end of	21,074	213
3	as well as	18,300	185
4	part of the	17,367	176
5	out of the	15,655	158
6	there is a	15,319	155
7	some of the	15,196	154
8	a number of	15,162	153
9	a lot of	14,652	148
10	there was a	14,356	145

As an example, the top ten in a list of three-word clusters from the British National Corpus World Edition (henceforward BNC) is given in Table 1. Raw frequency and normalised counts per million are given.[1]

We consider clusters to be of interest because they give insights into important aspects of the phraseology used by writers in specific contexts. As we commented in Chapter 2, we fully accept that they do not give anything like the whole story – especially as they do not provide insights into widely separated collocational patterns (e.g. Howarth 1996). However, our experience is that a study of cluster lists can offer insights to researchers, teachers, and learners. In particular, they can help build an understanding of an important aspect of how expert texts are formed, and the extent to which apprentice performances might coincide with or differ from these expert performances. As Howarth (1996) has shown, a systematic study of collocation in the academic writing of published and apprentice authors can help students to develop a fuller command of the style appropriate to their field. We feel that, in like manner, a study of clusters in relevant collections of texts has the potential to enhance our appreciation (and that of learners) of what works in particular kinds of text, and what has a better chance of being accepted by experienced readers in specific fields.

Resources

In writing this chapter, we have worked with a research corpus of MA dissertations written by students in the department of English Philology at the University of Pozńan in Poland,[2] the BNC World English Edition (henceforward BNC_ALL) and BNC-baby edition (Burnard 2004). For the MA material, we were initially provided with 21 dissertations, 16 with a literature focus, and 5 written by English language teaching majors. In order to tighten the focus of the study, we ended up only using the literature dissertations (352,258 words – henceforward POZ_LIT). As a reference corpora we used the 100 million words in BNC_ALL along with subsets from that corpus. These included a 500,000 word collection of literary studies periodical articles (BNC_LIT), along with three 1 million-word collections from BNC-baby – conversation (BNC_CONV), academic writing (BNC_ACAD) and prose fiction BNC_FICT).

Approach

Granger and Tribble (1998) have discussed the value of using collections of apprentice texts in writing instruction, and have stressed the importance of using relevant models (whether expert or apprentice) when helping apprentice writers to develop a control of a new genre. We are of a similar opinion, and also endorse Flowerdew's comment that:

> Many native speakers make use of others' writing or speech to model their own work in their native language where the genre is unfamiliar. It is time that this skill was brought out of the closet, and exploited as an aid for learning.
>
> (Flowerdew 1993:309)

Despite this endorsement of Flowerdew's overall position, we prefer not to use the terms "learner" and "native speaker" in studies of writing, and will use the terms "apprentice" and "expert". We consider apprentice texts as unpublished pieces of writing that have been written in educational or training settings, (often) for purposes of assessment. "Expert performances" (Bazerman 1994:131) are texts that are felt to be "situationally effective" (ibid.:23) by members of a particular discourse community. Expert texts may most easily be identified on the crude basis of their having been published, or their having been disseminated to specific readerships within bureaucratic, commercial, professional or other organisations.

In this chapter we will consider ways of describing the language used by highly proficient Polish apprentice writers working in a foreign language (English), and will argue for the systematic use of exemplars of relevant expert performances both in supporting apprentice writers and in informing the practice of teachers of writing. Such exemplars can provide a basis for the external and self evaluation of apprentice writing, and constitute a resource for helping writers as they work towards expertise.

The actual procedure used in this chapter will, by now, be familiar, and involves an interplay between the analysis of wordlists (and, on occasion, keyword lists), and the close review of the texts on which we are focussing. Again, as in earlier chapters, we try to approach the texts with as few pre-conceptions as possible, using frequency data as a starting point for identifying the features we will study, but always drawing on our experience of written communication to assess the salience of the features that are given prominence by the statistics.

Analysis 1: Clusters in academic writing in English

As an assessment of the overall value of working with clusters, we give below an account of contrast between the 100 million word BNC World Edition and the BNC_ACAD collection. Although Biber et al. (2000:990–1024) provide an extensive discussion of the major features of four word lexical bundles in conversation and academic writing, they do not (for obvious reasons) consider how these features operate in apprentice writing. The following discussion begins by comparing the top 20 single, two, three and four-word cluster lists for BNC_ACAD with the equivalent top 20s from BNC_ALL. This initial study demonstrates the value of cluster lists value in differentiating between different categories of text production, and serves as an exemplification of the methodology we will use when comparing apprentice and expert text. In subsequent sections in the chapter we will offer a specific account of the lexical bundles in our collection of apprentice texts.

Single word lists

For single words, the first thing you notice is that the top 20 lists for BNC_ALL and BNC_ACAD are very similar, with only four unshared items and with normalised counts (per million) being roughly the same. The differences (asterisked in the columns) are:

- *was, I, he, you*, and *at* in the BNC_ALL top 20 – absent from the academic prose
- the presence of *are, this, which, or* and *not* in the BNC_ACAD list.

We can account for the contrast in the case of personal pronouns, by recalling the prejudice against the use of the first person singular subject and second

Table 2. Wordlists (BNC_ALL vs. BNC_ACAD)

N	BNC_ALL	Norm.	BNC_ACAD	Norm.
1	the	61,205	the	66,732
2	of	30,825	of	41,975
3	and	26,526	and	25,348
4	to	26,275	to	24,986
5	a	22,046	in	23,951
6	in	19,666	a	21,923
7	that	10,636	is	16,525
8	is	9,848	that	11,824
9	it	9,326	be	8,899
10	for	8,904	for	8,844
11	*was	8,732	as	8,785
12	*i	7,403	it	7,798
13	on	7,391	*are	7,171
14	with	6,671	by	6,914
15	as	6,623	*this	6,699
16	be	6,586	with	6,639
17	*he	6,000	*which	5,722
18	*you	5,948	on	5,520
19	*at	5,297	*or	5,239
20	by	5,190	*not	4,936

person address in academic prose, and, more importantly, their centrality in dialogue (both real and in fictional representations). *He* may figure more widely in BNC_ALL both because of its importance in dialogue, but also because of the importance of male actors in a wide range of narratives (both scholarly and journalistic). What this says about the gendered nature of English language use in the late 20th Century is an issue beyond this present discussion.

In the case of the asterisked words in the BNC_ACAD list, we could predict that they are present because of the relative importance of anaphoric deixis in academic texts (frequently realised through *this*), and the need that writers have to link ideas through patterns of subordination and coordination (hence high frequency for *which* and *or*), and, in the case of *are*, and *not* the need for writers of academic texts to make statements concerning general truths. In the case of *at*, unlike the personal pronouns which do not occur until much lower down the list (*I* = 57, *you* = 139, *he* = 63), this string occurs at position 25 in the BNC_ACAD list so does not appear to be a significant discriminator.

Despite these limitations, it is already interesting to see how even a simple frequency sorted wordlist can help us to begin to understand contrast between sets of texts.

Two-word clusters

The two-word cluster lists for BNC_ALL and BNC_ACAD are also very similar (see Table 3 below – <u>non</u>-shared items are asterisked *). However, the prominence of *can be* in the BNC_ACAD list may be an indication of the contrasting importance of hedging in the academic texts, especially in view of their lower ranking in BNC_ALL (*can be* = 39). The prominence of existential *there is* in BNC_ACAD is notable. In BNC_ALL this is at position 36 and is preceded by *that's*, and *I'm*, giving an indication of the relative preference for informally expressed or personally oriented statement in BNC_ALL compared with BNC_ACAD.

The most likely explanation of the high frequency of *it+'s* in BNC_ALL is the frequent occurrence of the form in spoken language, representations of dialogue in prose fiction, and in journalistic registers.

Although these contrasts are of value when it comes to being able to distinguish the academic journal texts in BNC from a larger population, as we shall see, they are not so compelling as the contrasts obtained from a consideration of three-word clusters.

Table 3. BNC_ALL vs. BNC_ACAD – two-word clusters

BNC_ALL	Norm.	BNC_ACAD	Norm.
of the	7,695	of the	9,832
in the	5,252	in the	5,887
to the	2,941	to the	3,042
on the	2,243	it is	2,599
and the	1,996	and the	2,262
to be	1,915	to be	2,253
for the	1,696	that the	1,999
*at the	1,534	on the	1,988
it is	1,429	of a	1,953
by the	1,328	for the	1,574
*it was	1,325	by the	1,552
that the	1,320	*can be	1,401
with the	1,305	with the	1,362
*it 's	1,280	from the	1,324
of a	1,270	in a	1,323
from the	1,266	as a	1,275
in a	1,163	is a	1,172
as a	903	*is the	1,054
is a	796	*there is	1,011
*with a	794	*is not	982

Table 4. BNC_ALL vs. BNC_ACAD: Three-word clusters – shared

BNC_ALL	Norm.	BNC_ACAD	Norm.
a number of	153	a number of	260
as well as	185	as well as	252
in order to	122	in order to	181
one of the	360	one of the	261
part of the	176	part of the	231
some of the	154	some of the	233
the end of	213	the end of	159
the fact that	132	the fact that	200
there is a	155	there is a	286
there is no	118	there is no	233

Table 5. Frequency in BNC_CONV

RANK	BNC_CONV	Normalised count
none	a number of	0
none	in order to	0
118	the end of	114
410	some of the	58
636	part of the	44
723	there is a	40
949	the fact that	34
1,024	as well as	32
4,516	there is no	12

Three-word clusters

In contrast to the two-word cluster lists reviewed above, there is a marked difference between the three-word cluster lists for BNC_ALL and BNC_ACAD. Thus in the top 20, only 10 strings are shared in the three-word cluster (Table 4) and these shared items are themselves an interesting group as they are very strongly associated with written production, with very small representation in the collection of conversational English in BNC_CONV. The rankings of these three-word clusters (i.e. the position of a cluster in a list sorted for frequency from highest to lowest) in BNC_CONV are given in Table 5 along with their normalised counts.

Another major distinguishing characteristic of the list of unshared BNC_ACAD 20 three-word clusters (Table 6), is the absence of past time reference – present tense appears to be more important in academic texts.

Table 6. BNC_WR / BNC_ACAD: Three-word clusters – unshared

BNC_ALL	Norm.	BNC_ACAD	Norm.
out of the	158	in terms of	323
a lot of	148	it is not	244
there was a	145	per cent of	232
it was a	139	the number of	229
end of the	137	the use of	219
be able to	136	it may be	174
per cent of	122	in which the	173
I don't know	121	that it is	164
to be a	120	in this case	158
it would be	108	it has been	152

Four-word clusters

The top 40 tables for three-word and four-word clusters for BNC_CONV, BNC_ACAD and BNC_LIT are given below (Tables 7, 8) – all referenced against BNC_ALL. They offer insights into some important contrasts between the ways in which three-word and four-word clusters work. The shaded areas in each column indicate the three- and four-word clusters which are shared between BNC_ALL and each of the text collections under discussion. The smaller the shared area, the greater the contrast between the text collections.

At first sight, four-word and three-word clusters appear to be more or less equally useful as discriminators between conversational and written academic texts. Four-word clusters appear to be a little better at showing the contrast between the conversation collection and a large general collection of texts (there are no shared four-word clusters in the top 40s for BNC_ALL and BNC_CONV). However, there appears to be little difference between the value of four-word cluster and three-word cluster lists when comparing BNC_ACAD and BNC_LIT with BNC_ALL. Both are better than two-word clusters at separating the sheep of one kind of discourse from the goats of another.

However, there is an important difference between three and four-word clusters – and this is made clearer when we look at what Biber et al. (2000: 1015) call "noun phrase with *of*-phrase fragment". In the list of three-word clusters shared by BNC_ALL and BNC_ACAD we find combinations such as in Table 9.

Taking "one of the" as an example, in the four-word cluster list shared between BNC_ALL and BNC_ACAD the only instance containing this string is "one of the most". This is perfectly reasonable as there is a normalised count of 48 instances of this form in the BNC_ACAD collection; there are only 8 instances of the next *one of the* + forms (*one of the main*) in the collection.

Table 7. BNC_ALL vs. CV, AC and LIT: 3 word cluster lists compared

BNC_ALL	BNC_CONV	BNC_ACAD	BNC_LIT
a lot of	a lot of	a number of	as well as
be able to	be able to	as a result	at the end
i don't know	i don't know	as well as	at the same
it was a	it was a	in terms of	end of the
a number of	a bit of	it is a	in order to
as a result	a couple of	it is not	in terms of
as well as	a little bit	on the other	in the first
at the end	at the moment	one of the	it is a
at the same	but i mean	part of the	it is not
at the time	do you know	per cent of	one of the
end of the	do you think	some of the	out of the
have to be	do you want	that it is	part of the
in order to	don't know what	the end of	that it is
in terms of	four five six	the fact that	the end of
in the first	have a look	the use of	the fact that
it is a	have you got	there is a	the use of
it is not	i don't think	there is no	there is a
it was the	i don't want	to be a	there is no
it would be	i mean i	and it is	to be a
members of the	i think i	and so on	a sense of
most of the	i think it's	but it is	and in the
on the other	i want to	in order to	and it is
one of the	if you want	in relation to	as in the
out of the	it in the	in the case	but it is
part of the	no i don't	in this case	in the same
per cent of	no no no	in which the	in which the
some of the	one two three	it has been	is to be
that it is	that's what i	it is possible	it is the
that it was	three four five	it may be	of the poem
the end of	to do it	likely to be	of the world
the fact that	two three four	many of the	sense of the
the first time	what are you	shown in fig	some of the
the number of	what do you	terms of the	that of the
the rest of	what is it	that there is	the form of
the use of	yeah i know	the basis of	the nature of
there is a	you have to	the case of	the same time
there is no	you know i	the effect of	the work of
there was a	you know what	the house of	this is a
there was no	you want to	the number of	this is the
to be a	you've got to	the other hand	to have been

Table 8. BNC_ALL vs. CV, AC and LIT: 3 word cluster lists compared

BNC_ALL	BNC_CONV	BNC_ACAD	BNC_LIT
the end of the	a bit of a	as a result of	as well as the
at the end of	are you going to	as well as the	at the beginning of
at the same time	da da da da	at the end of	at the end of
for the first time	do you want a	at the same time	at the same time
on the other hand	do you want me	at the time of	at the time of
as a result of	do you want to	in terms of the	in terms of the
the rest of the	five six seven eight	in the case of	in the case of
per cent of the	four five six seven	in the context of	in the form of
in the case of	four one two three	in the form of	is one of the
one of the most	ha ha ha ha	it is possible to	it is possible to
the secretary of state	have a look at	on the basis of	on the other hand
by the end of	i don't know i	on the other hand	the end of the
is one of the	i don't know if	one of the most	the fact that the
to be able to	i don't know what	per cent of the	the rest of the
on the basis of	i don't know whether	the end of the	the way in which
i'm going to	i don't think so	the fact that the	a sense of the
in the middle of	i don't want to	the nature of the	and at the same
at the time of	i think it was	the rest of the	and it is a
as well as the	i thought it was	the way in which	as we have seen
in the form of	if you want to	a wide range of	as we shall see
the top of the	know what i mean	as shown in fig	as well as to
i think it's	mm mm mm mm	as we have seen	at the heart of
a member of the	no i don't think	can be used to	in so far as
the way in which	no no no no	in relation to the	in the course of
the fact that the	oh i don't know	in the absence of	in the work of
you've got to	one two three four	in the course of	it is hard to
a great deal of	or something like that	in this case the	it is in the
was one of the	six seven eight nine	is likely to be	it is true that
a wide range of	thank you very much	it is clear that	of the reality of
the middle of the	three four five six	it is difficult to	on the part of
the nature of the	three four one two	it is important to	one of the most
at the beginning of	two three four five	it is necessary to	seems to have been
will be able to	two three four one	more likely to be	that there is no
the back of the	well i don't know	on the part of	the extent to which
in terms of the	what do you mean	that there is a	the means by which
i'd like to	what do you think	that there is no	the nature of the
it is possible to	what do you want	the extent to which	the reality of the
secretary of state for	you don't have to	the size of the	the story of the
in the context of	you know what i	the structure of the	to be found in
as part of the	you want me to	the ways in which	to do with the

Table 9. "Of" phrase fragments

a number of	in terms of	one of the	part of the
per cent of	some of the	the end of	the use of

Table 10. Academic lexis

1	most	14	greatest	27	things
2	main	15	principal	28	basic
3	major	16	factors	29	leading
4	first	17	great	30	advantages
5	two	18	key	31	highest
6	few	19	many	32	last
7	reasons	20	largest	33	very
8	parties	21	central	34	chief
9	more	22	other	35	purposes
10	earliest	23	aims	36	authors
11	problems	24	fundamental	37	functions
12	three	25	four	38	important
13	best	26	following	39	ways
				40	difficulties

However, the top 40 right collocates of the three-word cluster "one of the" in a larger collection of academic texts (BNC Social Science) constitute an important set of terms which are imporant in academic discourse (Coxhead 2000) (Table 10).

The issue here is which information has the highest pedagogic value. Biber et al. comment:

> Three-word bundles can be considered as a kind of extended collocational association, and are thus extremely common. Four-word, five-word and six-word bundles are more phrasal in nature and correspondingly less common.
>
> (Biber et al. 2000:992)

While this is unquestionably the case, it begs the question of which data is going to be more useful to learners: an analysis limited to strongly phrasal elements, or one which includes "extended collocational associations" and which we feel offer learners a means of discovering a range of less frequent, but no less valuable phrasal combinations. *Most* may be by far and away the most frequent immediate right collocate of "one of the", but there is a wealth of other combinatorial potentials which we will lose sight of if three word clusters + their right collocates are excluded from our analysis.

Cluster lists – conclusion

A recent study by Cortes (2004) follows Biber and Conrad (1999) in arguing for the use of four-word clusters as a means for examining contrast between published and student written performances in specific disciplinary contexts (in her case, history and biology). She bases her argument on the premise that, inter alia:

> ... many four-word bundles hold three-word bundles in their structures (as in *as a result of*, which contains *as a result*).   (Cortes 2004: 401)

On the basis of our preliminary study, we would conclude, however, that while four-word clusters are strong discriminators between registers, there is a good argument for also using three-word clusters together with their immediate right collocates in studying the contrast between different styles of writing or the product of different groups of writers. And this is what we will do in the next part of this chapter.

Analysis 2: Clusters in apprentice texts

The Poznan literature MA dissertation corpus

As we said in the introductory comments, the main focus of this chapter is an account of a set of apprentice performances written by Polish MA students. Our purpose is to see if it is possible to identify the extent to which these apprentice works are similar to, or different from, expert performances in equivalent fields, and then to assess the extent to which this kind of description might have pedagogic value. The 16 texts in the collection[3] cover a wide range of literary critical topics – from social determinism in Shakespeare to the significance of Zen in the writings of the Beat Generation (see chapter Appendices). A randomly selected example of the quality of expression to be found in these apprentice performances can be seen in the extract in Figure 1.

This extract strikes us as being reasonably typical of the other texts in the corpus. Although we are dealing with a sophisticated writer addressing a complex topic, readers may identify infelicities that you would not expect to find in an edited expert performance. A selection of these (most of which jar on an experienced reader because they have very low probability) is given below, along with a more probable re-wording:

Sylvia Plath as a Poet of the Extremes: a Study of Father Figure, Nature and Death in her Writing.

Introduction

Sylvia Plath frequently wondered whether she lived to write or wrote to live. Everything she experienced, her stay in a mental hospital included, served her as a source of inspiration for her poems. Most of them seem to come straight from an actually suffering human being. A separation of her life and art is thus rather inadequate. Plath's poems share a confessional atmosphere and intensity and can be viewed as vivid reflections of her frames of mind at different stages of her short life. An all-embracing feeling of trauma and suffering can be traced in everything she committed to paper.

Poznan corpus: 1999-04-5_lit.txt

Figure 1. Poznan student writing example

- … *served her as a source of* inspiration for her poems (*served as a source of* – there are no occurrences of *served + personal pronoun + as* in BNC)
- Most of them seem to come straight from an *actually* suffering human being (*genuinely suffering* – all instances of *actually + suffering* in BNC occur as components of predicates – e.g. *she is actually suffering…*)
- A separation of her life and art is thus *rather inadequate* (*inadequate:* The only instances of *rather inadequate* in BNC occur as elements in noun phrases – e.g. *this rather inadequate data …*)

While such minor infelicities can be identified in the extract, we are not assuming that they are a major issue in the majority of the texts in the corpus, and they will not be an explicit focus of the study. Rather, we shall be assessing the extent to which there is evidence of any systematic similarity or contrast at the level of phrase structure between these apprentice performances and expert performances in the same academic field in BNC, and between these literary studies oriented texts and the BNC as a whole. The starting point for the discussion will be a list of three-word clusters in POZ_LIT. We will focus on the top 40 items, excluding proper noun clusters such as *Uncle Tom's Cabin* or *the Beat Generation*. This list, and a four-word cluster list from the same corpus (Table 11), are the key data sets we will work with in the rest of this chapter.

Comparing expert with apprentice academic writing

Our first concern has been to assess the extent to which the comparisons we make in the study are useful. We have already seen that written texts with contrasting contexts of production or more tightly specified communicative

Table 11. POZ_LIT three-word clusters – top 40

POZ_LIT-PN	Norm.				
as well as	427	it is the	203	he does not	132
in order to	363	to be a	184	out of the	132
one of the	337	it is not	158	part of the	132
the fact that	324	that it is	158	that he is	129
the same time	269	at the end	155	the process of	129
at the same	266	in which the	155	a number of	126
of the world	258	point of view	155	out to be	126
seems to be	255	to be the	155	end of the	124
of the novel	242	the world of	150	in the first	124
the end of	232	of the poem	147	it is a	124
on the other	219	the other hand	147	a kind of	121
there is no	213	the idea of	137	of the story	121
in the novel	208	the role of	134	the concept of	121
				the nature of	121

purposes (BNC_ALL / BNC_ACAD) display significant differences between the high-frequency three- and four-word cluster lists generated for them.

In the next stage of this study we will begin by comparing apprentice written performances with the whole BNC. Subsequently, we will refine the analysis in two stages. First we will compare the apprentice texts with general academic expert performances (as we find in the Academic Writing component of BNC Baby). Secondly we will compare the writing of the students in literary studies with expert writing in the same domain (fortunately there is a set of articles from literary journals in BNC).

Our first step, therefore, is to compare a three-word cluster list for the Poznan Literature MA scripts (henceforward POZ_LIT) with one derived from BNC_ALL. In the following discussion we will work with the top 40 clusters from three-word cluster lists generated with Wordsmith Tools 4. We will leave four-word clusters to a final discussion. We recognise that at just over a third of a million words, the POZ_LIT corpus is not large, but we do feel that it lets us reach illuminating conclusions. As before, normalised counts are used to facilitate comparisons with BNC_ALL.

The examples given below have been processed so that shared and unshared clusters are grouped. Each set has been alphabetically and numerically sorted to make relationships clearer, with the frequency column indicating counts in the original wordlist. The most frequent three-word cluster in BNC_ALL (*one of the*) occurred 35,603 times (normalised = 360); the most

Table 12. BNC_ALL vs. POZ_LIT – shared

BNC_ALL	Norm.	POZ_LIT	Norm.
a number of	153	a number of	126
as well as	185	as well as	427
at the end	107	at the end	155
at the same	81	at the same	266
end of the	137	end of the	124
in order to	122	in order to	363
in the first	82	in the first	124
it is a	100	it is a	124
it is not	105	it is not	158
on the other	86	on the other	219
one of the	360	one of the	337
out of the	158	out of the	132
part of the	176	part of the	132
that it is	83	that it is	158
the end of	213	the end of	232
the fact that	132	the fact that	324
there is no	118	there is no	213
to be a	120	to be a	184

frequent three-word cluster in POZ_LIT was *as well as*, and occurred 162 times (normalised = 427).

Table 12 shows the 18 three-word clusters that BNC_ALL and POZ_LIT share.

The majority of these clusters are implicated in the development of an argument, or reference to location (textual, temporal, or physical). The strikingly high normalised counts (normalised to counts per million) for *as well as*, *in order to*, and *the fact that* in POZ_LIT may merit further investigation. A real contrast does, however, emerge when concordances strings in the shared POZ_LIT / BNC_ALL three-word cluster lists are compared. This contrast concerns the ways in which frequent clusters are used in one collection when compared with the other. The following instances exemplify how *at the end* is used in as a means of referring to elements in texts in POZ_LIT.

> The defeat of Rupert, of good by evil, **at the end** of the book, is only an ambiguous victory for the comic realm of mechanical substitution and repetition.
>
> The embarkation foretold **at the end** of the play is also determined by Prospero's previous actions.

Table 13. Collocates of "at the end"

day	year	month	season	week	war	chapter
period	book	century	line	session	street	road
life	tunnel	term	meeting	corridor	years	summer

Table 14. BNC_ALL vs. POZ_LIT-PN

BNC_ALL	Freq.	Norm.	POZ_LIT	Freq.	Norm.
A lot of	14,652	148	a kind of	46	121
as a result	7,980	81	he does not	50	132
at the time	8,164	83	in the novel	79	208
be able to	13,408	136	in which the	59	155
have to be	7,608	77	it is the	77	203
I don't know	11,927	121	of the novel	92	242
in terms of	10,076	102	of the poem	56	147
it was a	13,718	139	of the story	46	121
it was the	7,867	80	of the world	98	258
it would be	10,641	108	out to be	48	126
members of the	7,980	81	point of view	59	155
most of the	8,660	88	seems to be	97	255
per cent of	12,029	122	that he is	49	129
some of the	15,196	154	the concept of	46	121
that it was	7,693	78	the idea of	52	137
the first time	7,689	78	the nature of	46	121
the number of	9,749	99	the other hand	56	147
the rest of	8,694	88	the process of	49	129
the use of	9,132	92	the role of	51	134
there is a	15,319	155	the same time	102	269
there was a	14,356	145	the world of	57	150
there was no	9,008	91	to be the	59	155

While the text related sense of *at the end* predominates in the small POZ_LIT text (story, book, poem, novel), this is not the case in BNC_ALL where temporal and spatial reference are the dominant right collocates. Table 13 gives all the nouns in the top 40 right collocates of "at the end". As this is one of the rare cases where a five-word cluster is strongly present (*at the end of the*) we will focus on the collocates immediately to the right of *of the*. Although *chapter* and *book* are present, they are not the dominant forms.

So far we have seen that POZ_LIT shares a number of high frequency three-word clusters with the full BNC corpus – although these clusters may occur in contrasting contexts.

Table 14 summarises the *unshared* three-word clusters in the top 40 three-word clusters for the two text collections.

The first notable feature of these lists is the occurrence in the POZ_LIT list of three-word clusters that are directly associated with textual reference. These have been marked in **bold** type in the table above. While it is possible to interpret these as simply the other half of *at the end* this would not be accurate as while there are only 59 instances of *at the end* in POZ_LIT, there is a combined total of 194 references to *of the novel, of the book* or *of the poem* in the three-word cluster list. The second important set of *of-phrase* fragments in this list is the group which refers to abstract entities like concept, idea, nature, process and role. These have been underlined in Table 14 above.

In comparing POZ_LIT with BNC_ALL it is important to remember that the contrasts we have noted for POZ_LIT are quantitatively similar to contrasts already noted between BNC_ACAD and BNC_ALL. Thus, BNC_ACAD top 40 shares 20 three-word clusters with BNC_ALL, and POZ_LIT top 40 shares 17 – many of which coincide with items on the BNC_ACAD list. There is, however, an important contrast as the set of 3-word clusters common to BNC_ALL, BNC_ACAD and POZ_LIT are not the same. Specifically, the three word clusters: *as a result / in terms of / per cent of / the use of /* and *there is a* are not to be found in the POZ_LIT top 40. We will return to this set in a later stage.

It now remains to be seen if there is any significant difference between POZ_LIT and BNC_ACAD. This review will help us to see the extent to which the linguistic behaviour of the Polish apprentice writers coincides with or differs from that of published expert writers. Having seen the extent to which the apprentice writers occupy shared ground with a general population of academic writers, we will then consider how their texts compare with expert performances in literary studies.

Comparing apprentice academic writing with general academic texts and expert texts in literary studies

We now move to a consideration of the extent to which the linguistic behaviour of the Polish apprentice writers (as exemplified at cluster level) coincides with or differs from that of published expert writers, both of a general academic population (BNC_AC) and in literary studies (BNC_LIT).

Set 1 puts together the three word clusters that are common to all three collections. Here we find a collection of clusters which are important in exemplification, argument development, and both internal and external reference.

Set 2 summarises those clusters which only appear in the top forty of BNC_LIT and POZ_LIT. As compared to the preceding set, these clusters are

Table 15. Common to BNC_ACAD, BNC_LIT and POZ_LIT

Set 1 (12 items)	as well as	in order to	in which the
	it is a	it is not	one of the
	part of the	that it is	the end of
	the fact that	there is no	to be a

Table 16. BNC_LIT and POZ_LIT only

Set 2 (10 items)	at the end	the nature of	of the poem
	end of the	at the same	out of the
	it is the	in the first	the same time
	of the world		

Table 17. BNC_ACAD and POZ_LIT only

| Set 3 (2 items) | a number of | the other hand |

Table 18. Top 40 three-word clusters: POZ_LIT, BNC_ACAD and BNC_LIT[4] – shared

Set 4 (6 items)	and it is		and it is
	but it is		but it is
	in terms of		in terms of
	some of the		some of the
	the use of		the use of
	there is a		there is a

more closely linked to the need to make reference to specific aspects of the parts or wholes of literary works or processes.

In the very small Set 3 the shared items are (significantly) both cliches – the risky generalisation *a number of* is a form many supervisors would advise students not to use, and *the other hand* is the second half of an over used double act.

By contrast, the 6 clusters (set 4) which the expert writers use and which are not present in the writing of the apprentices are either important in the construction of academic argument (especially *in terms of, the use of*) or typical of the neutral style which Biber (1988) (amongst others) associates with successful academic production.

An important observation stemming from these tables is that clusters which appear to be typical features of published academic prose are less common in the apprentice texts than in the expert performances. The strings that are common to BNC_ACAD and BNC_LIT but which are not present in the POZ_LIT top 40 are some of the most frequent three-word clusters in BNC_AC: *in terms of* and *there is a* are ranked 1 and 2, *some of the* is ranked 7.[5]

Secondly, POZ_LIT strings which are found in neither BNC_ACAD nor BNC_LIT top 40 (marked in **bold** in Table 19) may be seen as forming two groups. One includes items which can be accounted for by topic specificity – the kind of differentiating feature one would expect:

1.   *in the novel / of the novel / point of view / the concept of / the idea of / the process of / the role of / the world of*

Other clusters, however, may be more easily accounted for by viewing them as evidence of a naivety in the writing style of the apprentices. These include:

2.   *a kind of / on the other / out to be / seems to be*

A summary of these unshared clusters is given in Table 19 below.

Table 19. Top 40 three-word clusters: POZ_LIT, BNC_ACAD and BNC_LIT – unshared

BNC_ACAD (20)	POZ_LIT (16)	BNC_LIT (12)
and so on	**a kind of**	a sense of
as a result	**he does not**	and in the
in relation to	**in the novel**	as in the
in the case	**of the novel**	in the same
in this case	**of the story**	is to be
it has been	**on the other**	sense of the
it is possible	**out to be**	that of the
it may be	**point of view**	the form of
likely to be	**seems to be**	the work of
many of the	**that he is**	this is a
on the other	**the concept of**	this is the
per cent of	**the idea of**	to have been
shown in fig	**the process of**	
terms of the	**the role of**	
that there is	**the world of**	
the basis of	**to be the**	
the case of		
the effect of		
the house of		
the number of		

BNC_LIT vs. POZ_LIT – mapping similarity and difference: Three-word clusters

An analysis of the 21 shared three-word clusters and 19 eight unshared clusters in BNC_LIT and POZ_LIT top 40 is given in Table 20. They have been categorised using the classification adopted by Biber et al. (2000) in their treatment

Table 20. BNC_LIT vs. POZ_LIT: Shared and unshared clusters

Category	Shared	Unshared POZ_LIT	Unshared BNC_LIT
noun phrase with of-phrase fragment	the end of	a kind of	a sense of
	the nature of	a number of	in terms of
	of the poem	of the novel	sense of the
	of the world	of the story	some of the
	one of the	point of view	that of the
	end of the	the concept of	the form of
	part of the	the idea of	the use of
		the process of	the work of
		the world of	
		the role of	
noun phrase with other post-modifier fragments	the fact that		
prepositional phrase with embedded of-phrase fragment	*none present*		
other prepositional phrase (fragment)	at the end	in the novel	and in the
	at the same	on the other	as in the
	in the first		in the same
	in which the		
	out of the		
anticipatory it + verb phrase / adjective phrase	it is not		and it is
	it is the		but it is
	it is a		
	that it is		
passive verb + prepositional phrase	*none present*		
copula be + noun phrase / adjective phrase			this is a
			this is the
(verb phrase) + that-clause fragment	*none present*		
(verb / adjective) + to-clause fragment	in order to		is to be
	to be a		to have been
adverbial clause fragment	*none present*		
pronoun / noun phrase + be	there is no	that he is	there is a
other expressions	as well as		the same time

of lexical bundles. *Unshared* tri-grams have also been included in this analysis – thereby making it possible to see more clearly the nature of the contrasts between the two text collections.

This analysis makes it possible to see a number of contrast in the kinds of structures that the apprentice writers in POZ-LIT use compared with the expert performances in BNC_LIT. In particular, we can now see that in *noun phrase with of-phrase fragments* the apprentice writers have tended to use combinations that have a literal reference (e.g. *of the novel, of the story*), or which are less likely to occur as fixed phrases (the concept of, the idea of, the process of, the world of). The expert writers, by contrast, have tended to use combinations that are more likely to be used phrasally (e.g.: *a sense of, in terms of,*

cluster	BNC_CONV	Norm.	BNC_ACAD	Norm.
in terms of	5	5	338	319
the use of	5	5	230	217
the form of	0	0	109	103
the work of	0	0	80	75
a sense of	0	0	29	27

Table 21. "A kind of" in POZ_LIT

```
black lovers. His plantation is a    kind of a harem. Such portrait of a
). The protagonist functions in a    kind of a psychological void where
alt with the child who lives in a    kind of a symbiotic relation with i
t through politics, but through a    kind of aesthetic and psychological
chizophrenic state. She assumes a    kind of alter ego, "Elly Higginbott
, either of which would provide a    kind of answer to his question, but
dominate the male. I see man as a    kind of artifice, and woman as a ki
, horror and revulsion, and has a    kind of barbaric quality. Seen in t
re forces objectively served as a    kind of compensation for a deeply i
om and ultimately emanate with (a    kind of magic.( Like Conchis, who i
The Magus's god, emanates with (a    kind of magic;( Frederick Clegg, th
, contrary to European ones, as a    kind of marriage between a metropol
 for her. She and Dr Reefy form a    kind of mystical union based on "so
eling that David is undergoing (a    kind of ordeal.( Williams feels (a
His goodness does not stem from a    kind of organic unity between man a
at of the other characters - is a    kind of parody of this vulgar view
m seems to be, thus, for Lennie a    kind of personal religion. His word
er too full of mystery. This is a    kind of realistic version of The Ma
 kind of artifice, and woman as a    kind of reality. The one is cold id
ng, which again needs a head as a    kind of resonance box" (Christensen
priori some destructive power, a    kind of some negative energy. Marga
 trade, each of them performing a    kind of symbolic action representin
e can be regarded as a triumph, a    kind of "transcendence" of his fate
tive, nonrational id stands for a    kind of transcendent honesty and in
```

the form of, the use of, the work of), which are common or very common in BNC_ACAD, but which are either very rare or not present in BNC_CONV.

Conversely, in the unshared three-word clusters that can be found in POZ_LIT *a kind of* (see the concordance in Table 21) offers a good example of usage more commonly associated with speaking than with writing. Its normalised count is 121 in POZ_LIT, as compared with 25 per million in BNC_LIT, and, while none of the instances below are in any sense errors, there are alternative forms (e.g. *variety of, form of, type of*) that the apprentice may wish to be able to deploy as they mature as writers within the discipline.

POZ_LIT	BNC_LIT	POZ_LIT	BNC_LIT
and at the same	and at the same	as a result of	a sense of the
as well as the	as well as the	but at the same	and it is a
at the beginning of	at the beginning of	by the fact that	as we have seen
at the end of	at the end of	for the first time	as we shall see
at the same time	at the same time	for the sake of	as well as to
in the case of	in the case of	goes west to meet	at the heart of
is one of the	is one of the	in the course of	at the time of
on the other hand	on the other hand	in the first place	in so far as
one of the most	one of the most	in the light of	in terms of the
the end of the	the end of the	in the novels of	in the course of
the fact that the	the fact that the	is not able to	in the form of
the rest of the	the rest of the	of the fact that	in the work of
		of the novel is	it is hard to
		on the basis of	it is in the
		on the one hand	it is possible to
		seems to be the	it is true that
		the author of the	of the reality of
		the beginning of the	on the part of
		the characters of the	seems to have been
		the image of the	that there is no
		the point of view	the extent to which
		the protagonist of the	the means by which
		the role of the	the nature of the
		the same time he	the reality of the
		the time of the	the story of the
		to the fact that	the way in which
		turned out to be	to be found in
		turns out to be	to do with the

Figure 2. POZ_LIT vs. BNC_LIT: Four-word clusters

BNC_LIT vs. POZ_LIT – mapping similarity and difference: Four-word clusters

To complete this comparison of expert and apprentice, we will apply the same mapping process to four-word clusters in POZ_LIT and BNC_LIT. The four-word cluster lists are given in Figure 2 (shared clusters are in the shaded columns) followed by the analysis.

An immediate contrast between the three-word and four-word cluster lists is that they indicate a smaller amount of common ground between the two text collections with only twelve shared items. As clusters containing proper nouns were removed from both lists, this indicates a noticeable contrast between the phrasal orientation of the two sets of writers. An analysis will be provided for each major section.

Analysis 1

There are more *of-phrase fragments* in POZ_LIT than in BNC_LIT and they have a physicality in their reference that is largely absent in BNC_LIT. Where the POZ_LIT clusters refer to *novel, author, beginning, characters, image, protagonist, role,* the small number[6] of *of-phrase fragments* refer to *sense, reality, nature* and *story*. This contrast could provide a starting point for research into contrasts between the ways in which apprentice and expert writers in literary studies engage with their subject matter.

Category	Shared	Unshared POZ_LIT	Unshared BNC_LIT
noun phrase with of-phrase fragment	is one of the one of the most the end of the the rest of the	of the fact that of the novel is the author of the the beginning of the the characters of the the image of the the point of view the protagonist of the the role of the the time of the	a sense of the of the reality of the nature of the the reality of the the story of the

Analysis 2

While there are no noun phrases with other post-modifier clusters in the top
40 lists, there is a contrast between the unshared lists of prepositional phrases
with embedded of-phrase fragments. The smaller number of these items in the
apprentice texts (with one having physical reference – *novel*), is not the main
difference. More importantly, in the seven clusters in the BNC_LIT unshared
list we find evidence of the means used by the expert writers to make relations
between the texts they are considering and other referents in a world beyond
these texts. The concordance lines below give an indication of the resources
that the expert writers are able to draw on in making these connections. On
the basis of the evidence from the cluster analysis, we have no evidence of the
apprentice writers making links of this kind.

```
ams, scorning to think of them in terms of actual reincarnations, though th
is simply describing one thing in terms of another, then the case for a Chr
one, interpreted by being seen in terms of Antony's meeting with Cleopatra
ench or Anglo-Norman fabliaux? In terms of basic structure there is no doub
 erring personality is defined in terms of breadth and contrast; the effect
hing like a political novelist in terms of British domestic politics, and h
y called it God, understood it in terms of Christian theology and used the
e itself becomes inconceivable in terms of clocks and calendars. Shredding
gs that are generically wrongs in terms of conventional Christian morality
 myrrh. But it is conventional in terms of Eliot's earlier poetry; though l
s the issues of life and death in terms of everlasting and perishable goods
). Note the I. He was thinking in terms of first-person narrative --; Raskol
abliaux to supply their wants, in terms of food, sex and entertainment, by
n which can also be thought of in terms of gesture. James Harris, writing i
```

Category	Shared	Unshared POZ_LIT	Unshared BNC_LIT
noun phrase with other post-modifier fragments	none present	none present	none present
prepositional phrase with embedded of-phrase fragment	at the beginning of at the end of in the case of	in the light of in the novels of for the sake of on the basis of	in terms of the at the heart of at the time of in the course of in the form of in the work of on the part of

Analysis 3

In the case of other prepositional phrase fragments, the ratio is reversed, with unshared POZ_LIT containing six of these clusters as opposed to one in un-shared BNC_LIT. Also, significantly, the only shared cluster in this category is *on the other hand* – in itself an interesting case, as in the British English of BNC_ALL (in contrast to POZ_LIT) we find this pair not to be a pair. Table 22 summarises this contrast.

In the full BNC *on the other hand* is a lexical bundle in Biber's terms (>20 per million words), but *on the one hand*, with 14 counts per million, is not. In BNC_ACAD, both are lexical bundles, but *on the one hand* is at the lower limit of the range (26 per million) and well outside the top 40 at rank 55. In the apprentice text, although *on the other hand* is still the more frequent of the pair (an extrapolated 147 per million), *on the one hand* is much closer (84 normalised counts) and well inside the top 40 at position 12. What appears to be happening with this group of clusters is that the apprentice writers view *on the one hand* and *on the other hand* as a pair, and use them in combination. This contrasts with the behaviour of expert writers, who make use of *on*

Category	Shared	Unshared POZ_LIT	Unshared BNC_LIT
other prepositional phrase (fragment)	on the other hand	by the fact that but at the same for the first time in the first place on the one hand to the fact that	in so far as

Table 22. On the one hand / on the other hand

Rank		Freq.	Norm.
	BNC_ALL		
5	on the other hand	5,312	54
87	on the one hand	1,419	14
	BNC_ACAD		
1	on the other hand	131	124
55	on the one hand	28	26
	POZ_LIT		
2	on the other hand	56	147
12	on the one hand	32	84

the other hand to introduce a contrast, without feeling an obligation to use an introductory form.

Analysis 4

The contrasting uses of *anticipatory it* and *that-clause* fragments is one of the most striking in the analysis of four-word clusters. Biber (1988) demonstrated the importance of *anticipatory it* in the construction of formal writing. The significance of this contrast does not only lie in the fact that the apprentice writers used these structures less than the experts. Perhaps more significantly, *anticipatory it* is also strongly implicated in the evaluations which the expert writers offer (*hard, possible, true*). While there is a total of 36 instances of structures such as those below across the expert collection, there are only 3 instances in the apprentice texts.

Category	Shared	Unshared POZ_LIT	Unshared BNC_LIT
anticipatory it + verb phrase / adjective phrase		and it is a	it is hard to it is in the it is possible to it is true that
passive verb + prepositional phrase	*none present*	*none present*	*none present*
copula be + noun phrase / adjective phrase	*none present*	*none present*	*none present*
(verb phrase) + that-clause fragment	the fact that the		that there is no

Analysis 5

Contrasts between *to-clause* fragments and *adverbial clause* fragments are less marked. The apprentice use of "turns/ed out to be" seems to be a strategy which all the apprentice writers use when they wish to present a summarising conclusion in relation to character or action in the texts they are discussing. Contrast between the *adverbial clause fragments* used by the different writers focuses on the use or non-use of *we* in anaphoric and cataphoric referencing of different stages in a developing argument. In fact, the only four-word clusters containing *we* which have any significance of occurrence are *that is why we* and *in this way we,* neither of which have this discourse organising function.

Category	Shared	Unshared POZ_LIT	Unshared BNC_LIT
(verb / adjective) + to-clause fragment		is not able to seems to be the turned out to be turns out to be	seems to have been as well as to
adverbial clause fragment	and at the same at the same time	as a result of	as we have seen as we shall see
pronoun / noun phrase + be	*none present*		
other expressions	as well as the	the same time he goes west to meet	

Identifying contrast between apprentice and expert performances – An interim conclusion

If the analysis that has been undertaken in this chapter had been developed as a pedagogic account of a set of apprentice writing, it would only be part of the story. Clearly, with the information to hand, we have no means of evaluating the apprentice texts that we have been discussing (nor the expert texts for that matter). However, we have seen that there are discernible differences between the text collections in question, and that some of these differences may indicate that the apprentice writers are offering a less sophisticated account of what goes on in literary texts than that offered by the published expert writers. For example, the low use of *anticipatory it* four-word clusters in the apprentice texts may point to there being less evaluation in the apprentice dissertations, or it may point to the fact that evaluation is being done in a different but equally appropriate way. Likewise, the apparently descriptive orientation of the apprentice texts as evidenced by *noun phrase with of-phrase fragment* three-word clusters may indicate a lack of sophistication in the analysis – or it may not.

This is not to deprecate the value of the analysis that has been undertaken. After all, we have made life difficult for ourselves by taking apprentice texts which have been accepted for submission at MA level in a prestigious Polish English Philology department. You do not find much better than this in any environment where English is used for academic purposes. What we feel this discussion has shown, is that an analysis of clusters in comparable text collections can be helpful in identifying areas where writers may wish to extend the range of what they can do by comparing their own performances with writing that they aspire towards. We also feel that we have demonstrated the value of using both three-word and four-word clusters when considering apprentice texts. While four-word clusters do indeed give insights into strongly phrasal dimensions of the texts, three-word clusters may give richer insights into a broader range of phenomena that will be of value in helping learners to develop a wider expressive repertoire.

Notes

1. The total word count for BNC World edition excluding header information is given as 98,931,968 by Wordsmith Tools 4.

2. The dissertations were kindly provided by Dr. Prezmysław Kaszubski (School of English, Adam Mickiewicz University, Poznan, Poland).

3. 361,335 words. Longest = 39,040, shortest = 11,564. Mean = 22,583.

4. In each of the examples for the literary studies collections, proper nouns have been removed. Curiously this made no overall difference to the numbers of items between BNC_LIT and POZ_LIT – only altering the composition of the unshared item lists.

5. *Of the reality of* and *the reality of the* are part of a five-word cluster *of the reality of the*.

Appendix – BNC texts

BNC-baby Academic Texts

A6U	CLP	EWW	HRG
ACJ	CLW	F98	HWV
ALP	CMA	F9V	HXH
AMM	CRS	FC1	J18
AS6	CTY	FEF	J57
B17	EA7	FPG	J7G
B1G	ECV	FSS	
B2K	EW1	FT1	

BNC-baby Demographic Conversation

KB5	KCC	KD8	KP5
KB7	KCF	KDD	KP7
KBC	KCU	KDF	KPU
KBD	KCV	KDJ	KPX
KBH	KD0	KE2	KSN
KBJ	KD1	KE4	KSW
KBP	KD3	KNR	
KBW	KD7	KP2	

BNC-baby Literary Fiction

AB9	CDB	G0S	HR9
AC2	CFY	G0Y	J10
BMW	FAJ	GUU	J54
BPA	FET	GVL	K8V
C8T	FPB	H85	
CB5	G01	H9C	
CCW	G0L	H9D	

BNC Literary criticism

A18	CAW	A1A	A05
A1B	CKN	CFX	HXS
A6B	CRV	APS	HY6

Poznan literature dissertation titles

Anglo-Saxon culture in Przekrój – its role in the breaking of cultural barriers in the years 1949–1959.

Buddhism and the Literature of the Beat Generation.

Elizabeth Bishop and Wislawa Szymborska Read Through Simone Weil's Writings.

Exhaustion and Replenishment. The Concepts of Language in Samuel Beckett's The Trilogy and Paul Auster's The Invention of Solitude and The New York Trilogy.

Individual vs society: the social determination of character's choice in selected tragedies and tragicomedies by Shakespeare.

Modes of Historical Representation in the Fiction of E. L. Doctorow: Ragtime and The Book of Daniel.

Pre- and post-civil war reaction to Uncle Tom's Cabin.

Psychoanalytic reading of Angela Carter's selected works.

Sylvia Plath as a Poet of the Extremes: a Study of Father Figure, Nature and Death in her Writing.

The Concept of Godgame in William Shakespeare's The Tempest and John Fowles's fiction.

The concept of women's writing as illustrated in the Handmaid's Tale and The Robber Bride by Margaret Atwood.

The Constant of Transcendentalism in American Literature.

The decline of moral values in the selected novels by Iris Murdoch, Muriel Spark and William Golding.

The lonely crowd – human alienation in a metropolis in selected American novels of the 1950s.

The Meaning of Protean Character in John Barth's The Sot-Weed Factor and Herman Melville's The Confidence Man.

Two Fictions of the Self: Paul Auster's The New York Trilogy and Moon Palace.

## CHAPTER 9

What counts in current journalism

Keywords in newspaper reporting

Summary

In this chapter we consider ways in which Keyword analysis can be used to build an understanding of the major themes which have been addressed by a contemporary, quality British newspaper, the Guardian Weekly, during the period 1996 to 2001. In carrying out this analysis we also see how Keywords can help us better understand the kinds of evaluations that journalists and editors make as they construct a news agenda, and, despite the significant progress that has been made in the UK in the area of gender equity, how there still appears to be a major imbalance to the space given to the reporting of the actions of men as opposed to those of women. In a final part of the chapter we show how Keywords can be used in a diachronic study to identify the leading themes for each year of the newspaper corpus.

Introduction

Newspaper language is widely used in a range of education contexts: from reading passages in language course books, to forming a core resource in historical, social, and cultural studies. Fowler (1991) has shown how a linguistic analysis can contribute to a better understanding of the ideological and cultural construction of news stories, and many others, including Fairclough (1989), Stubbs (1996), and Bell (1999), have presented approaches to analysing and describing how newspaper language constructs social realities. Biber (1989) and Biber et al. (2000) have also used newspaper corpora to demonstrate the systematic grammatical contrasts between the lexico-grammar of this major register of written language and the lexico-grammar of registers such as academic writing, prose fiction and conversation.

In this chapter, we will use Keyword analysis to help us to consider newspaper language from three perspectives. First, we will use Keywords to show some of the main themes that are covered by a particular British newspaper (The Guardian), and how these themes are presented in this particular publication. We will then use Keyword analysis to consider gender balance in UK news reporting, and finally, will show how Keyword analysis can reveal the shifting news agenda of the Guardian during the period 1996 to 2001.

Resources

The main resource that has been used in the development of this chapter is a 14,317,898 word archive of articles from the weekly edition of the UK newspaper, the Guardian.[1] Subscribers to the newspaper can receive a weekly email version of the paper that is subdivided into the sections: UK News, US News, International News, Sport, Culture, and Features.[2] The archive we have worked with here is subdivided on the same basis. The UK News section – the major focus of the study – contains 1,865,767 words. The breakdown in terms of words per year is given in the table below:

1996	90,804
1997	420,387
1998	397,236
1999	381,027
2000	330,797
2001	237,045

The smaller numbers of words in the 1996 and 2001 collection are because the archive compilation began after the beginning of 1996, and the latest version we were provided ran to September 2001.

The other major resource we have drawn on, as in other chapters, is the British National Corpus, both in its International and Baby versions.

Approach

In this instance, we had no specific hypothesis to test, other than a general assumption that newspaper language differs in some respects from other kinds of writing and that newspaper editors make selections from what they *could* report, when deciding what they *will* report. All that we were interested in was finding out as much as we could about what is happening in this collection of newspaper articles. The approach could be used by teachers and students of languages or with a media-studies interest, historians, or other social researchers. At first sight this might seem insufficiently rigorous, a weak, "suck it and see" attitude with no clear focus. On the contrary, we would argue that to look at a set of texts in descriptive mode wanting first to see which patterns can be found there is a proper procedure for research. The Keywords procedure usually generates a list some of whose members immediately arouse insights and cry out for further analysis. In the last analysis, the proof of the pudding is in the eating and readers will have to judge for themselves whether this study produces insightful findings or otherwise.

Analysis 1: Who, what, where?

Who?

Given below is a list of the top 100 Keywords for all sections of the Guardian weekly for the period 1996–2001 (Table 1). When reviewing this list it is important to bear in mind that it brings together the words that have the greatest statistical prominence when compared with the reference corpus.

If a Keyword list for the sports pages of the Guardian Weekly is generated, it looks completely different – the top 20 Keywords for such a list are given in Table 2 as an example.

In the sports section of the newspaper, football and motor racing dominate, along with the results (# = any number in the text), – yet they cannot challenge the political figures of the period when it comes to the totality of the newspaper. The focus of the reporting in the newspaper is fixed on a very small number of key players and countries. Given that the Guardian weekly is a leading British newspaper, it is not surprising that the names of the Prime Minister of the day and the leader of the main opposition party are high on the list, but it is revealing that it is the name of the US President at that time, and the capital city of that country are the most prominent Keywords in the list.

Table 1. GW vs. BNC Keywords

1.	Washington	26.	year	51.	month	76.	Pinochet
2.	Clinton	27.	nations	52.	Chinese	77.	victory
3.	last	28.	China	53.	Euro	78.	reviewed
4.	president	29.	Israeli	54.	Russian	79.	army
5.	has	30.	former	55.	Beijing	80.	Paris
6.	Blair	31.	co	56.	campaign	81.	Netanyahu
7.	anti	32.	American	57.	leaders	82.	Putin
8.	U.S.	33.	countries	58.	Taliban	83.	rebels
9.	United	34.	political	59.	Americans	84.	against
10.	international	35.	Palestinian	60.	British	85.	Timor
11.	EU	36.	leader	61.	corruption	86.	UK
12.	Mr	37.	self	62.	crisis	87.	his
13.	news	38.	Milosevic	63.	Gore	88.	weapons
14.	Kosovo	39.	minister	64.	human	89.	Hague
15.	post	40.	European	65.	Prime	90.	billion
16.	government	41.	non	66.	said	91.	Blair's
17.	war	42.	peace	67.	world's	92.	UN
18.	States	43.	global	68.	its	93.	sanctions
19.	world	44.	Russia	69.	ethnic	94.	violence
20.	military	45.	rights	70.	years	95.	Serbian
21.	NATO	46.	election	71.	Africa	96.	GM
22.	who	47.	Bush	72.	country	97.	African
23.	internet	48.	Israel	73.	Ms	98.	refugees
24.	officials	49.	Clinton's	74.	US	99.	Iraq
25.	Britain	50.	foreign	75.	Palestinians	100.	rightwing

Table 2. GW_sports vs. BNC Keywords

N	Keyword	N	Keyword
1	#	11	football
2	cup	12	Arsenal
3	England	13	game
4	victory	14	won
5	final	15	team
6	match	16	Schumacher
7	win	17	after
8	Premiership	18	United
9	second	19	last
10	ball	20	minutes

A Keyword list, then, can give us an immediate view of which personalities are dominating the news agenda of a specific newspaper over a particular period. In the case of the Guardian weekly 1996–2001, these people were:

2	Clinton
6	Blair
38	Milosevic
47	Bush
49	Clinton's
63	Gore
76	Pinochet
81	Netanyahu
82	Putin
89	Hague
91	Blair's

This list is of itself significant as it summarises the heroes, villains and supporting cast in the period immediately before the 11th September attack on the World Trade Centre in New York, from this newspaper's perspective. If, however, you had no knowledge of the period, how would you be able to sort the good guys from the baddies?

The most effective means of answering this question is found by reviewing the collocates of each Keyword. As an example, we will take the cases of Clinton, Blair and Milosevic.

Second step – Check the immediate collocates

Apart from discovering why there is such a large number of Clinton and Blair entries – Hillary and Cherie have independent news interest – our clue regarding the evaluation that the newspaper has made of the these three heads of state can be found in the terms it uses to describe the legal structures they lead. For President Clinton it is an *administration* or a *presidency*, for Prime Minister Blair it is a *government*, but for President Milosevic it is a *regime*. Regime is a word in English which has what Louw (1993) has called "negative semantic prosody"; i.e. it is a word that tends to associate itself with negative evaluations. Sinclair (2003:18) considers the word in KWIC concordance context and suggests similar conclusions. This view is confirmed by a review of the immediate left collocates of *regime* in the BNC (see Table 4 below), where we find a litany of the contemporary and historical demons of the western powers. In contrast, in the left collocates of *government* we find largely neutral adjectives and

Table 3. Clinton, Blair, Milosevic – collocates

Clinton		Blair		Milosevic	
Left	Right	Left	Right	Left	Right
the	administration	Tony	and	Slobodan	and
President	and	Mr	has	Mr	to
Bill	has	the	is	the	is
Mr	said	news	said	of	has
that	was	that	was	that	the
Hillary	is	and	to	with	was
with	to	for	the	for	in
for	in	with	had	to	who
of	administration's	to	in	President	regime
and	had	a	*will*	against	*will*
to	the	of	who	and	that
by	who	as	government	on	had
Mrs	*will*	Mrs	as	Belgrade	but
news	last	Cherie	last	by	as
as	did	white	told	as	may
a	presidency	by	on	news	for
said	as	what	would	anti	of
when	on	which	should	if	said
but	Gore	between	also	while	he
against	for	Macaskill	a	Steele	a

proper nouns (most frequently country names). The implication is clear. If we exclude fiscal matters, *regimes* are run by *them* – the dictators, war mongers and political pariahs. *Governments* are what *we* and our allies have.

What and where?

Returning to our Keyword list (Table 1), it is also possible to identify the dominant themes for the period in question. Although there are some pre-dictable (and important) candidates for consideration, including: *Kosovo, internet, peace, global* and *GM*, a non-intuitive instance of the value of Keywords is provided by #7, *anti*. A review of the collocates of *anti* gives an immediate view of the issues that dominated news reporting between 1996 and 2001. The top twenty are given in Table 5.

Each of these words can be further analysed by considering its wider collo-cational associations. *Semitism* and *semitic* are exceptional cases, as, effectively, they only occur in the context of *anti*.[3] For this part of our study, we will, therefore, focus on Keyword #3, *corruption*. Our method has been to search

Table 4. Regime / government: Immediate left collocates

Regime – left		Government – left	
Afghan	Nazi	Local	Regional
Ancien	Noriega	Central	Chinese
Apartheid	Nom Penh	Labour	Minority
Authoritarian	Regulatory*	British	Irish
Castro	Repressive	Conservative	Soviet
Ceausescu	Safety*	Federal	Party
Communist	Smith	National	State
Fascist	Socialist	Coalition	Military
Franco	Soviet	UK	Iraqi
German	Spanish	US	Italian
Iranian	Special	French	Spanish
Iraqi	Strict*	German	Russian
Kabul	Tax*	Anti	American
Marxist	Tsarist	Interim	Democratic
Military	Vat*	Tory	African
Najibullah	Vichy	Provisional	Israeli
		Thatcher	Indian
		Japanese	Socialist
		Transitional	Cabinet

Table 5. GW "anti" collocates

	Word	#		Word	#
1.	semitism	113	11.	apartheid	44
2.	semitic	73	12.	American	62
3.	corruption	74	13.	aircraft	41
4.	globalisation	67	14.	immigration	37
5.	ballistic	60	15.	missile	95
6.	drug	81	16.	nuclear	34
7.	government	77	17.	poverty	29
8.	personnel	59	18.	war	40
9.	communist	64	19.	AIDS	26
10.	terrorist	51	20	mafia	23

for *corrupt**, thereby obtaining the full lemma of the word, and to set a wide horizon for collocates (10 left and 10 right). We have then selected the top 20 nouns that occur in the listing of total collocates. These are given below in Table 6 with the total counts in the right hand column.

Here we find that *governments* and *police* are the institutions the Guardian Weekly most associates with corruption in its various forms, and that *presidents* appear to be more prone to temptation than other classes of political leader.

Table 6. Corrupt* collocates

1.	government	95	11.	public	33
2.	police	90	12.	crime	32
3.	officials	80	13.	scandal	32
4.	system	46	14.	state	32
5.	officers	43	15.	trial	30
6.	party	41	16.	being	29
7.	power	41	17.	economic	29
8.	president	41	18.	military	28
9.	scandals	41	19.	international	27
10.	politicians	38	20.	country	26

Although *corruption* occurs in the context of *public / state / economic / military* and *international*, the only specific geographical collocates that occur above a threshold of nine occurrences are:

UK	12	American	9	London	9	Nigeria	9
British	12	Beijing	9	Mexican	9	Paris	9
United States	11	Britain	9	Mexico	9		

Although this data is slightly skewed as *UK* occurs as a part of the heading of sections of the newspaper text (see example concordance lines below), it is not misleading, as the *corruption* reported nevertheless occurs in Great Britain.

```
age 10 UK News / Yard targets corruption / Duncan Campbell Ya
UK News / Oxbridge accused of corruption on subsidies / John
ek ending , Page 10 UK News / Corrupt police are 'working the
eek ending , Page 7 UK News / Corruption swoop on elite polic
e 9 UK News / War declared on corrupt police / Duncan Campbel
/ Met police officers in anti-corruption drive Met police off
ch 29, 1998, Page 9 UK News / Corrupt police face fast-track
ing , Page 8 UK News / Police corruption growing Police corru
K News / Labour MP cleared of corruption / Gerard Seenan Labo
```

Analysis 1: Conclusion

So far we have seen that we can use Keywords to identify major themes in the news reported by a single newspaper. This approach can be used in comparative studies of the ways in which the press within a single country or internationally deal with specific issues. Keyword analysis is not restricted to such theme focused work. As we shall see in the next section, it can also be used in a broader cultural analysis.

Analysis 2: It's a man's world – gender balance in the Guardian Weekly's news reporting

The Keyword list in Table 1 above has already shown us that the major players in the news agenda of 1996 to 2001 appear to be men: *Blair / Blair's / Bush / Clinton / Clinton's / Gore / Hague / Milosevic / Netanyahu / Pinochet / Putin.* Although we have seen that Hillary Clinton and Cherie Blair were standing in their husbands' shadows, the overall picture from the top 100 Keywords is that the people who count in the news are men. This impression is reinforced when we consider that unlike *she* and *Mrs* which do not occur in the top 100 Keywords, *Mr* (position 12) and *his* (position 87) are both in the top 100 – though Ms does occur at position 73. This is not to say that *she* is not a frequent word in the GW corpus (it is at position 68 in the full wordlist, although *he* is at position 17!). The occurrence of *Mr* and *his* in the Keyword List underscores how prominent they are in the corpus when it is compared with the larger BNC collection.

To investigate the issue of gender balance, we have, therefore, two immediately available resources: Keyword lists and wordlists. The Keyword list demonstrates significant contrasts between the research corpus and the reference corpus. Wordlists can be used to further investigate relative distributions of terms across text collections, and can also be a starting point for the investigation of the environments in which these terms occur. In the rest of this section we will consider what insights a study of *titles* and *pronouns* in the GW corpus can provide.

Titles

The main gendered titles we will review are *Mr, Ms, Mrs,* and *Miss.* The first information we have about them is their relative distribution in the GW and BNC corpus (Table 7).

Table 7. Titles in GW and BNC

GW	total =	13,996,358	BNC	total =	97,367,611
N	Word	Norm	N	Word	Norm
62	Mr	1619	138	Mr	679
1,381	Mrs	81	464	Mrs	216
787	Ms	141	4,624	Ms	19
2,549	Miss	43	850	Miss	122

Table 8. miss vs. Miss

	GW	Norm	BNC	Norm	BNC-baby (NEWS)
miss	375	27	3138	32	51
Miss	221	16	8638	89	77

The striking contrast here is how much more frequently *Mr* occurs in the GW corpus compared with BNC. When the counts are normalised to counts per million, GW has nearly three times as many instances of *Mr* than has the BNC. Interestingly, although the counts for *Mrs* and *Ms* show strong contrast between the two corpora, when the scores are combined (GW = 222 // BNC = 235) we find that there is an almost equal count in the two collections. This indicates that a house style decision has been made by the Guardian Weekly to adopt *Ms* as a general female title, a decision that is also reflected in the contrast between *Miss* in GW (normalised count: 43) and *Miss* in BNC (normalised count: 122), although this will also be influenced by the large proportion of instances of non-title *miss* in each corpus. If, however, the raw results are separated into the title and non-title forms (easily done by carrying out a case sensitive sort on a concordance for *MISS* and checking for (the very rare) instances of sentence initial non-title *MISS*. The final picture for *MISS* is as in Table 8.

This new perspective gives us further confirmation of the strong divergence between GW and BNC. While BNC has 89 instances per million of this title form, GW only has 16. As a confirmation of the contrast, we reviewed the Newspaper component of BNC-Baby. Here there are 128 total instances of *MISS* (normalised count). Of these, 51 are non-title *miss* with the remaining 77 being title *Miss*. Again, a much greater frequency when compared with the Guardian Weekly, and an indication of change across the last decade of the twentieth century. The extent to which the Guardian is ahead of a trend is another question,[4] and could form the basis for a useful further study.

So far we have seen that there is a dramatic contrast between the frequency of female specific titles and the single male title commonly in use in English. The total "female" and "male" title counts for GW and BNC are:

Table 9. Total Female vs. Male titles in GW & BNC

GW	Count	Norm	BNC	Count	Norm
total F	3,699	264	total F	34,759	357
total M	22,661	1619	total M	66,114	679

Given that the ratio of male:female titles is greater than 6:1 in GW, compared with a ratio of just less than 2:1 in BNC, there would seem to be a massive predominance of the reporting of things related to male actors or patients over the reporting of their female counterparts in this particular newspaper during this period.

Pronouns

As a way of extending this analysis, it is possible to use a list of the gendered personal pronouns that exist in English. In the next stage of the study we will review the occurrences of *he, him, his, she, her,* and *hers* in the GW corpus. We would predict that there will be a greater occurrence of male compared with female.

The results support this prediction – although the contrast is not quite so dramatic at approximately 4:1 male:female pronoun occurrences. We found this contrast a little surprising as we had thought that the male pronouns might be being used as gender neutral terms in contexts such as in Table 10.

Where we do find a dramatic contrast is in the collocates of these items – particularly the right collocates. The complete table for the top 50 immediate right collocates for male and female pronouns is given in Table 11.

This has been analysed in terms of three simple categories: family related words, verbs, all other nouns. The remaining terms have been ignored for the purposes of this analysis. Results will be discussed below. In the following tables, the first column (#) indicates the keyness rank of a word in collocates list for the make and female pronoun sets, the *c1 / c2* columns indicate the class a word has been ascribed to, and *Norm* gives the count normalised to counts per million.

Table 10. Male:Female pronouns in GW

Word	Norm	Word	Norm
she	1,353	he	5,414
her	1,640	him	1,011
hers	6	his	4,980
TOTAL FEMALE	3,000	TOTAL MALE	11,404

Table 11. Male / female pronouns: Immediate right collocates

FEMALE

1 ↘

was	would	can	told	head
is	life	did	does	wrote
said	mother	a	husband's	made
had	father	as	she	body
has	first	also	home	children
husband	family	son	new	two
own	in	daughter	face	with
to	could	work	went	didn't
says	will	parents	for	writes
and	the	death	became	sister
				↘50

MALE

1 ↘

was	and	a	party	became
said	will	added	way	home
is	could	as	work	career
had	wife	can	death	wants
has	did	told	second	he
own	also	family	may	for
would	life	does	wrote	might
to	the	took	new	or
says	in	made	went	son
first	father	mother	should	with
				↘50

Table 12. GW: Male / female family word right collocates

#	MALE	c1	Norm	#	FEMALE	c2	Norm
14	wife	f	73	6	husband	f	40
20	father	f	49	13	mother	f	23
26	family	f	36	14	father	f	22
30	mother	f	30	16	family	f	18
49	son	f	24	26	son	f	11
				27	daughter	f	10
				29	parents	f	10
				33	husband's	f	9
				45	children	f	7

Table 13. GW: Male / female – nouns

#	MALE	c1	Norm	#	FEMALE	c2	Norm
17	life	n	56	12	life	n	24
31	party	n	30	28	work	n	10
33	work	n	29	30	death	n	10
35	death	n	27	35	home	n	8
42	home	n	25	37	face	n	8
43	career	n	25	41	head	n	7
				44	body	n	7

Discussion 1: Family words

While there is a balance between the prominence given to respective spouses in the lists, we find that the female pronouns have a much larger share of family related nouns in their immediate right contexts than do the male. On the evidence here, 9% of the total instances of *her* have a family word as immediate right collocate, but only 4% of the instances of *his* have this kind of collocate.

Discussion 2: Nouns

As with the case of family words, male and female pronouns share some common ground in the top 50 list of immediate right collocates: the rich set of *life, work, death, home.* However, while men and women have some shared experience, there are important divergences. These are evidenced by the list for men having *party* ranked higher than all the other noun collocates apart from *life,* and *career* occurring 25 times in every million words. Women, in contrast, appear to have neither parties nor careers, but, notably, do seem to be concerned with *face, head,* and *body* in ways which men are not. Although the Guardian may be a liberal paper, its reporting would still seem to be involved in the construction of a world in which women are defined by familial relations and their appearances, while men are engaged in a world of political parties and careers. True, men and women live and die and have homes, but they appear to do their living and dying in different contexts.

Discussion 3: Verbs

So far as verbs are concerned, there are few contrasts in these to lists – apart from men doing all of these things more frequently per million words, and

Table 14. GW: Male / female – verbs

#	MALE	c1	Norm	#	FEMALE	c2	Norm
2	said	v	408	3	said	v	86
9	says	v	111	9	says	v	36
22	added	v	43	31	told	v	9
25	told	v	41	38	went	v	8
28	took	v	32	42	wrote	v	7
37	wrote	v	27	43	made	v	7
39	went	v	27	49	writes	v	6
44	wants	v	24				

also seeming to *add* things to their statements, and to *want* things more than women do.

Analysis 2: Conclusion

We have now seen how a Keyword list can give an insight into how large classes of individuals are treated in news reporting. By focusing on words that have little or no lexical content of themselves, it is possible to build an appreciation of how the classes of individuals represented by those words are represented in a newspaper.

Analysis 3: A changing world – UK news 1996–2001

As a final step in this consideration of the use of Keywords in an analysis of the Guardian Weekly, we will look at how the news agenda has shifted over the period for which we have data (1996–2001). To carry out this study we have taken advantage of the structure of the GW archive and have made six separate Keyword lists for the UK news sections of each year. Two Keyword lists have been made for each year, one referenced against the BNC, the other against the GW corpus. This has been done so that it is possible to see what is prominent in a year in relation to a large population of texts, and what uniquely prominent in the UK news sections when compared with the rest of the Guardian Weekly.

We give two views of the data below. Table 15 shows the top 5 words in each year of the UK News section between 1996 and 2001. Table 16 is an alphabetically sorted list of the top 20 for each year. This view makes it easier to identify shared and unshared high frequency items.

Table 15. GW UK News: Top 5

1996	1997	1998	1999	2000	2001
MR	LABOUR	MR	MR	MR	MR
TORY	MR	BLAIR	LABOUR	SAID	SAID
LABOUR	BLAIR	LABOUR	LORD	BRITAIN	BRITAIN
SIR	TORY	LORD	BLAIR	BLAIR	RAILTRACK
WILLETTS	MPS	LORDS	STRAW	LABOUR	POLICE

Table 16. GW UK News: Top 20 (alphabetic)

1996	1997	1998	1999	2000	2001
BIRT	BLAIR	BLAIR	BLAIR	BLAIR	**ANIMALS**
CLARKE	BRITAIN	BRITAIN	BRITAIN	BRITAIN	**ASYLUM**
COMMITTEE	BRITISH	COMMONS	BRITISH	BRITISH	BLAIR
COMMONS	**ELECTION**	FEIN	FAYED	**DOME**	BRITAIN
CURRENCY	FEIN	FOR	**GM**	GOVERNMENT	COWAN
DUNBLANE	IRA	GOVERNMENT	HEALTH	HEALTH	**DISEASE**
HAMILTON	LABOUR	**IRA**	**IRA**	INQUIRY	DOCTORS
HANDGUNS	LABOUR'S	LABOUR	LABOUR	JAMES	**FOOT**
HOWARD	LORD	LORD	LONDON	LABOUR	IRA
INQUIRY	MAJOR	LORDS	LORD	LEWIS	JAMES
LABOUR	MILLION	MILLION	LORDS	LIVINGSTONE	LABOUR
LORD	MP	MINISTERS	MPS	LONDON	LEWIS
MICHAEL	MPS	MPS	MR	LORD	LONDON
MILLION	MR	MR	SAID	MR	LORD
MPS	SAID	MULLIN	SCOTTISH	**NHS**	**MOUTH**
MR	SECRETARY	SAID	SECRETARY	REPORT	MR
SIR	SINN	SECRETARY	SINN	SAID	POLICE
TORY	SIR	**SINN**	STRAW	SECRETARY	**RAIL**
WHIP	TORIES	ULSTER	TORY	STRAW	**RAILTRACK**
WILLETTS	TORY	WILL	ULSTER	WOULD	SAID

UK News top five – GW_UK_NEWS vs. BNC

Purely on the basis of these 30 words we can begin to construct an account of the events and players with the highest profile in the Guardian Weekly's reporting of the UK over the period for which we have data. Adopting the position of a hypothetical visitor from Mars (with a minimum awareness of British history) we would be able to report:

–   Men (MR) dominated the agenda, and that many of these men were concerned with the LABOUR and TORY parties.

- The man (presumably a politician) who dominated the years 1997 to 2000 was called BLAIR, although other people with the names WILLETS and STRAW were also significant players
- Although Britain is a parliamentary democracy, a lot of time was spent talking about people with the titles LORD or SIR, or the activities of the LORDS collectively, but that after 1999 this tendency diminished.
- The year 2001 contrasts strongly with the other years under consideration as both POLICE and RAILTRACK enter the top 5 for the first time.

UK News top twenty

The alphabetically sorted top 20 list of keywords for each year takes us directly to the heart of the news agenda for each year. In the table below, the Martian visitor has ignored the names of people this time and focused on a small number of high frequency nouns that have proven to be worth considering following a review of concordances.

With no prior knowledge of the UK, the visitor from the red planet has been able to make the following time-line for UK history:

1996	1997	1998	1999	2000	2001
An attack on a school in Scotland (DUN-BLANE) causes an intense national debate on the use of HAND-GUNS	The Labour party lead by Tony Blair wins the general ELECTION of 1997. One of Labour's first priorities is to obtain a settlement with the IRA in Northern Ireland	The IRA and peace talks in Ireland continue to be a focus of attention	GM (genetically modified) crops are to be trialled in the UK in the face of protests from a large environmental lobby. The IRA continues to be a problem	In the run up to the Millennium, the government gets bogged down in a problematic prestige project to build an exhibition DOME. At the same time there is a crisis in the National Health Service (NHS)	Although this is an election year (which Labour wins) the main issues in the news are ASYLUM seekers, FOOT and MOUTH disease of ANIMALS, and major problem with the RAILways that are run by RAILTRACK.

Conclusion

In this chapter, we have seen how Keywords can be used to gain an insight into the ways in which news is reported in a major UK quality newspaper, and how the paper itself constructs that news agenda. We have also identified an apparently very large gender imbalance across the articles which appear in the Guardian – a surprise given the liberal profile of the paper. We have not, however, compared this newspaper with other publications, so are not in a position to say where the Guardian would be placed in gender bias league table!

What we hope is now clear is that (in combination with a carefully constructed corpus) it is possible to move from a purely descriptive account of language use in a particular social context, to the formation and testing of hypotheses regarding how and why language is used in particular ways within the text collection.

Notes

1. Used here with the kind permission of the editor of the Guardian Weekly, Max de Lotbiniére.

2. For more information visit http://www.guardian.co.uk/guardianweekly/emailservices/

3. 243 instances out of 245 in GW.

4. The Guardian has a reputation as a strongly liberal publication, and one which supports language usage that is sensitive to the needs and interests of women (amongst others).

## CHAPTER 10

Counting things in texts you can't count on

A study of Samuel Beckett's *Texts for Nothing, 1*

Summary

In this final chapter we consider the ways in which corpus tools which are usually used in the analysis of very large collections of texts can be of use in a study of a very short, short story. Following approaches which have their roots in literary stylistics, we show that an appreciation of a literary text can be strengthened through the use of ordinary office applications and specific text analysis tools such as wordlists and concordancers. These tools can be used to test our intuitive responses to a piece of literary writing and to reveal text structure and narrative development, as well as patterned unreliability in a narrative text.

Introduction

In earlier chapters in this book we have been mainly concerned with the study of large collections of texts. In this final chapter, both by way of a change, and also to emphasise the value of corpus tools in the analysis of whole texts, we will be looking at a single, very short, short story. We will also be looking at a literary text rather than, as has been the case with most of the instances drawn on thus far, texts which purport to refer to a real world – what Rossner and Widdowson (1983) calls *referential* texts, rather than those which attempt to *represent* a world.

Tribble and Jones (1990) discussed ways in which *Texts for Nothing, 1* (Beckett 1967) could be used as a resource for language teaching and learning. Here, we propose to return to this same story in order to demonstrate some of the ways in which the tools we have considered in earlier chapters (mainly wordlists, collocation lists and concordances) may also be of use to literary scholars. The text is useful from a teaching perspective because it is very short (1,546 words) and, despite its modernity, is surprisingly accessible to students. From a literary perspective, it is interesting its own right, being one of a set of widely regarded short stories, a complex and ambiguous text by a major figure in 20th century writing in English.

While the linguistic analysis of literary texts has a long and distinguished tradition (Chatman 1975; Leech 1969; Leech & Short 1981; Widdowson 1975, 1992) few, if any, scholars appear to have considered the ways in which computational tools can be applied to a single very short text. However, the use of statistical procedures of one kind and another in literary exegesis has a respectable tradition. As Halliday comments in his essay on Golding's *The Inheritors:*

> ... numerical data on language may be stylistically significant, whatever subsequent operations are performed, there has nearly always been some counting of linguistic elements in the text, whether of phonological units or words or grammatical patterns ... A rough indication of frequencies is often just what is needed: enough to suggest why we should accept the writer's assertion that some feature is prominent in the text, and to allow us to check his statements. The figures, obviously, in no way constitute an analysis, interpretation or evaluation of the style.   (Halliday, M. A. K. 1973:116–117)

It is this "rough indication of frequencies" which interests us in the case of *Texts for Nothing, 1.* What we hope to show in this chapter is that a reader's response to a text can be warranted by doing some counting – by identifying elements in the text which have *prominence* and then assessing their *salience* in an account of the work. As we have seen, text analysis software such as Wordsmith Tools can greatly facilitate the counting side of things. Interpreting the results of such an analysis – identifying salience – remains the task of the reader. This the machine cannot do for us.

Resources

The text

Texts for Nothing, 1 is a first person, narrative. In the original text it is 5 pages / 1,558 words long. The text is unparagraphed and from the outset establishes a fragmented, panting tone:

> Suddenly, no, at last, long last, I couldn't any more, I couldn't go on. Someone said, You can't stay here. I couldn't stay there and I couldn't go on. I'll describe the place, that's unimportant, The top, very flat, of a mountain, no, a hill, but so wild, so wild, enough. Quag, heath up to the knees, faint sheeptracks, troughs scooped deep by the rains. It was far down in one of these I was lying, out of the wind. Glorious prospect, but for the mist that blotted out

everything, valleys, loughs, plain and sea. How can I go on, I shouldn't have
begun, no, I had to begin.   (Beckett, S. 1967:71)

For those of you who have read Beckett, the story is familiar, a voice in extreme
conditions comments on a past that does not bear reflecting on too closely,
and engages (or fails to engage) with a present which may offer few dependable
consolations. The setting is a timeless Ireland, hence the *Quag, heath up to the
knees, faint sheeptracks, troughs scooped deep by the rains.*

Tools

The present study used three main software tools. Microsoft Word and Microsoft Excel, and Wordsmith Tools. While the first pair of programs provide
ways of counting crude text units – words and orthographic sentences – and
of then presenting this information in graphic form, WordSmith provides the
tools we need to study lexis, phrase structure and collocational patterns in more
systematic ways.

Analysis 1

The starting point for the analysis of the text was an attempt to account for
various impressions one of us had had as a reader. The first was that the story
has a two-, or possibly three-, part structure – and this structure is not simply a
beginning, middle, end of conventional narrative, but represents a transition
from one state to another. This relates to the second impression, the feeling that the opening of the story is "dark/negative", while later sections are
"light/positive". The third impression also relates to this overall structure, with
the feeling that in the course of the narrative the story shifts from alienation to
reconciliation. As text analysts, we are also interested in something else. This is
the question of the extent to which our desire for textual pleasure, for harmony
and reconciliation, conditions our initial response to the text. Are we really using the evidence that the text offers us, or imposing an interpretation which
may or may not be warranted?

In order to test the initial intuitions and to elaborate a more objective account of *Texts for Nothing, 1*, our first task was to convert the text into a file
which could be handled electronically. In the present instance, this involved
typing the text on a word-processor – although the option of scanning and
then processing with an Optical Character Recognition (OCR) software was

also available. Once the text existed as a plain text (ASCII) file it was possible to begin to work on it.

The first step in this process was to break the text down into sentence units. This can be done easily in any version of MS Word by searching for "sentences" (i.e. text blocks terminating with a full-stop) and reformatting the sentences so that each begins on a new line. In this instance, a number tag was then automatically allocated to each sentence using the Bullets & Numbers feature. The words in each sentence were counted (by marking the sentence as a block and then using the Tools/Word count feature). This re-structured, quantified text now looks as in Figure 1.

Once these basic units had been counted the sentence length data was transferred to Excel where the spreadsheet's capacity to represent numerical information graphically was exploited. The results of this first analysis are given (the vertical axis indicates sentence length in words, the horizontal axis indicate the graphemic sentences in the text) in Figure 2.

Sentence	Text	Count
\<s1\>	Suddenly, no, at last, long last, I couldn't any more, I couldn't go on.	14
\<s2\>	Someone said, You can't stay here.	6
\<s3\>	I couldn't stay there and I couldn't go on.	9
\<s4\>	I'll describe the place, that's unimportant.	6
\<s5\>	The top, very flat, of a mountain, no, a hill, but so wild, so wild, enough.	16

Figure 1. Sentence view

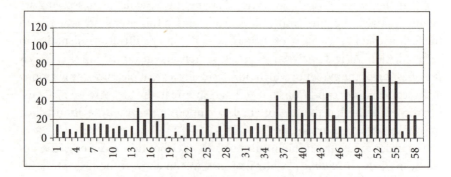

Figure 2. Texts for nothing 1: Sentence length

The pattern which immediately struck us is the apparent existence of at least four main "blocks" in the story. These are marked by the occurrence of very short sentences: #19 / #43 / #56 which come soon after a "peak" of contrastingly very long sentences: #16, #41and #52. There does appear to be, then, a quantifiable pattern of crescendo, and sudden diminuendo, but this does not necessarily coincide with the perception of "stages" in the narrative that we mentioned above. However, what we found from a closer reading of these long sentences and there contexts, does give some grounds for viewing them as change points or *pivots* in the development of the narrative.

Pivot 1

Sentence	Text	Count
#16	I am far from all that wrangle, I shouldn't bother with it, I need nothing, neither to go on nor to stay where I am, it's truly all one to me, I should turn away from it all, away from the body, away from the head, let them work it out between them, let them cease, I can't, it's I would have to cease.	64

Figure 3. Pivot 1

Sentence #16 can be seen as ending a first phase – the narrator is *far from all that wrangle*, at an impasse in which both body and head have ceased to be dependable –

> ... like an old hack foundered in the street, struggling no more, struggling again, till it gives up. I say to the head, Leave it alone, stay quiet, it stops breathing, then pants on worse than ever.

This said, there is also a note of uncertainty in the (parenthetic) comment *I should turn away from it all* ... And is there (another?) voice which adds its own subverting commentary on the decision? – *I can't, it's I would have to cease.*

Pivot 2

In a similar way, sentence #41 and #42 (linked as they are by *and*) seem to mark the end of another phase in the narrative – a phase which began at sentence #39 with the repeated question, *What possessed you to come?*, and its response: *unanswerable, so that I answered* and the subsequent replies to that question. The new phase is signalled by the last clauses of #42 *I can't go, I can't stay, let's see what happens next* – and so the narrative continues.

Sentence	Text	Count
#39	And that other question I know so well too, What possessed you to come? unanswerable, so that I answered, To change, or, It's not me, or, Chance, or again, To see, or again, years of great sun, Fate, I feel that other coming, let it come, it won't catch me napping.	51
#40	All is noise, unending suck of black sopping peat, surge of giant ferns, heathery gulfs of quiet where the wind drowns, my life and its old jingles.	27
#41	To change, to see, no, there's no more to see, I've seen it all, till my eyes are blear, nor to get away from harm, the harm is done, one day the harm was done, the day my feet dragged me out that must go their ways, that I let go their ways and drag me here, that's what possessed me to come.	63
#42	And what I'm doing, all important, breathing in and out and saying, with words like smoke, I can't go, I can't stay, let's see what happens next.	27

Figure 3. Pivot 2

Pivot 3

#52	Sometimes it's the sea, other times the mountains, often it was the forest, the city, the plain too, I've flirted with the plain too, I've given myself up for dead all over the place, of hunger, of old age, murdered, drowned, and then for no reason, of tedium, nothing like breathing your last to put new life in you, and then the rooms, natural death, tucked up in bed, smothered in household gods, and always muttering, the same old mutterings, the same old stories, the same old questions and answers, no malice in me, hardly any, stultior stultissimo, never an imprecation, not such a fool, or else it's gone from mind.	111

Figure 5. Pivot 3

Sentence #52, the longest sentence by far, can be taken as marking the beginning of the final phase of the story. Following some of the shortest, and most contradictory statements in the text – *I won't be afraid of the big words any more, they are not big*, they work with bleak humour (*nothing like breathing your last to put new life in you*) to prepare the reader for the final theme which is introduced in sentence #53:

> Yes, to the end, always muttering, to lull me and keep me company, and all ears always, all ears for the old stories, as when my father took me on his knee and read me the one about Joe Breem, or Breen, the son of a lighthouse keeper, evening after evening, all the long winter through.   (Beckett, S. 1967: 74)

Here we enter a fourth and final section in the text in which a reader can identify an appearance of harmony, an appearance of reconciliation.

Analysis 2

In the first part of this analysis, we saw that a crude text dimension such as sentence length could be used to identify what appear to be transitional moments in a short text. Having access to an electronic version of the document it was possible to use business tools (a spread-sheet and word-processor) to reveal structural patterning in wording of a literary text in a way which would have been impractical otherwise. In this second analysis, we shall use the dedicated text processing features of WordSmith Tools to test these initial insights by a consideration of other patterning in the text.

Wordlists and keyword lists

Table 1. Wordlist – *Texts for Nothing, 1*

THE	90	5.8%	WITH	13	0.8%
I	67	4.3%	GO	12	0.8%
AND	38	2.5%	ON	12	0.8%
TO	37	2.4%	OR	12	0.8%
IT	34	2.2%	NO	12	0.8%
IN	29	1.9%	ONE	12	0.8%
ALL	29	1.9%	WAS	12	0.8%
MY	24	1.5%	HAVE	11	0.7%
ME	24	1.5%	THAT	11	0.7%
OF	22	1.4%	SO	11	0.7%
A	17	2.2%	CAN'T	10	0.6%
FOR	16	1.0%	NOT	10	0.6%
HERE	14	0.9%	BE	10	0.6%
WHAT	14	0.9%	IS	10	0.6%
IT'S	13	0.8%	SAME	10	0.6%

If this book is about anything, it is about wordlists. In Chapter 2, the features of wordlists were discussed – mainly with a focus on large text collections. Even though in this instance we are working with a very short text, a wordlist still provides the best starting point for an analysis. Table 1 lists the most frequent items ($\geq$ 10) in *Texts for Nothing, 1*.

In themselves these items tell us little (although as we have seen, in other contexts and with other purposes, such a list can be an invaluable basis for –

for example – differentiating between contexts of production or authorship studies). What this list does provide, however, is a starting point for a study of words which may be of interest – the elements of the text that are *prominent*. As we have also seen, prominent can be more brought into sharper focus if a keyword list is generated. Such a list is given in Table 2, alongside a keyword list for the one million word BNC Baby Fiction reference corpus.

Table 2. Keyword lists – *Texts for Nothing, 1,* referenced against BNC_B_Fiction + BNC_B_Fiction

N	Texts for Nothing	%	N	BNC literature	%
1	THE	5.80	1	HE	1.74
2	I	4.32	2	SHE	1.17
3	AND	2.45	3	HER	1.04
4	TO	2.39	4	HAD	1.09
5	IT	2.19	5	WAS	1.62
6	ALL	1.87	6	HIS	0.95
7	IN	1.87	7	HIM	0.50
8	ME	1.55	8	ADAM	0.09
9	MY	1.55	9	SAID	0.54
10	OF	1.42	10	CORBETT	0.06

Unlike the keyword lists we have seen so far, that for *Texts for Nothing, 1* has no nouns in the top 10, but instead, and surprisingly, has THE as the first keyword. We have no immediate explanation for this, but our intuition is that this is either a feature of keyword lists for very short literary texts or reveals a contrast between the proportion of nouns in *Texts for Nothing* compared with the texts in BNC Baby Fiction. The presence of "I" (and ME and MY) is more easily accounted for – the story is a first person narrative, in contrast with the texts in BNC Baby.

In the next section we will focus on the prominent personal pronoun "I", seeing to what extent the contextual information that the concordancer provides can enable us to assess the *salience* of these features for the literary development of the text.

Concordances and keywords

The moment the concordance for "I" is generated, the relationship between the transitions which we have intuited, the textual patterning which we have identified through our account of sentence length, and a number of highly significant shifts in the narrative become strikingly obvious. The concordance for

"I" is given below in text sequence, It has been divided into the four major sections which we have already identified through the earlier analysis. Sentence numbers are given in <angle brackets>. The power of the concordancer is that it has isolated this prominent keyword and then transformed the text so that we can see the node both in relation to its vertically related equivalents *and* its immediate horizontal co-texts. This literal unpacking of the text enables us to begin to understand how our initial response to the story was formed. We will comment on the four different parts of the story in the discussion below.

PART 1

```
o, at last, long last,  I couldn't any more, I couldn't go on.    <s1>
, I couldn't any more,   I couldn't go on. <2> Someone said, You   <s1>
u can't stay here. <3>   I couldn't stay there and I couldn't go   <s3>
ouldn't stay there and   I couldn't go on. <4> I'll describe the   <s3>
  I couldn't go on. <4>  I'll describe the place, that's unimport   <s4>
r down in one of these   I was lying, out of the wind. <8> Glori   <s7>
n and sea. <9> How can   I go on, I shouldn't have begun, no, I h  <s9>
. <9> How can I go on,    I shouldn't have begun, no, I had to beg  <s9>
uldn't have begun, no,   I had to begin. <10> Someone said, perh   <s9>
ssed you to come? <11>   I could have stayed in my den, snug and   <s11>
  my den, snug and dry,   I couldn't. <12> My den, I'll describe   <s11>
couldn't. <12> My den,   I'll describe it, no, I can't. <13> It'   <s12>
  I'll describe it, no,   I can't. <13> It's simple, I can do not  <s12>
n't. <13> It's simple,    I can do nothing any more, that's what y  <s13>
s what you think. <14>   I say to the body, Up with you now, and   <s14>
, Up with you now, and   I can feel it struggling, like an old ha  <s14>
till it gives up. <15>   I say to the head, Leave it alone, stay   <s15>
```

Figure 6. Part 1

In Part 1, "I" is subject for a negated verb form in 7 out of 15 instances, and on other occasions where the verb form is positive (s4, s9, s13, s14) it is associated with an immediately following negation or a negative evaluation (e.g. *struggling like an old hack* – s14). Our sense of a "dark" beginning to the story would appear to have been constructed through this mainly past tense account of blocked or failing decisions and actions. The transition between Part 1 and Part 2 is signalled at the beginning of Sentence 16 by the statement: "I am far from all that wrangle".

Part 2 is mainly present time oriented (21 out of 31 lines). These are numbered and marked in the concordance. We have included *I wouldn't see* because it is a conditional rather than past habitual form, and *I can't have been here long* + *I wouldn't have held out* because of the past in the present reference.

The sequence between s16 and s39 is also marked by the much greater certainty of the statements the narrator makes. *I am far from all that wrangle,*

```
PART 2
worse than ever. <16>    1.I am far from all that wrangle, I s    <s16>
rom all that wrangle,    2.I shouldn't bother with it, I need    <s16>
ldn't bother with it,    3.I need nothing, neither to go on no    <s16>
 on nor to stay where    4.I am, it's truly all one to me, I s    <s16>
  truly all one to me,   5.I should turn away from it all, awa    <s16>
 them, let them cease,   6.I can't, it's I would have to cease    <s16>
  cease, I can't, it's   7.I would have to cease. <17> Ah yes,    <s16>
es, with a telescope,    8.I could see it from here. <23> It's    <s22>
s not just tiredness,    9.I'm not just tired, in spite of the    <s23>
b. <24> It's not that   10.I want to stay here either. <25> I     <s24>
tay here either. <25>    I had heard tell, I must have heard t   <s25>
25> I had heard tell,    I must have heard tell of the view, t   <s25>
e, come with me? <28>   11.I am down in the hole the centuriee    <s28>
 in a graveyard. <30>   12.I can't raise my eyes to them, whai    <s30>
to them, what a pity,   13.I wouldn't see their faces, their p    <s30>
 gone, sickened. <33>   14.I listen and it's the same thoughte    <s33>
t's the same thoughts   15.I hear, I mean the same as ever, se    <s33>
same thoughts I hear,   16.I mean the same as ever, strange.      <s33>
y. <35> How long have    I been here, what a question, I've of   <s35>
ere, what a question,    I've often wondered. <36> And often I   <s35>
dered. <36> And often    I could answer, An hour, a month, a y   <s36>
ry, depending on what    I meant by here, and me, and being, a   <s36>
 and being, and there    I never went looking for extravagant    <s36>
agant meanings, there    I never much varied, only the here wo   <s36>
seem to vary. <37> Or    I said, I can't have been here long,    <s37>
vary. <37> Or I said,   17.I can't have been here long, I wou     <s37>
 have been here long,   18.I wouldn't have held out. <38> I h     <s37>
t have held out. <38>   19.I hear the curlews, that means clo     <s38>
d that other question   20.I know so well too, What possessedt    <s39>
unanswerable, so that    I answered, To change, or, It's not m   <s39>
s of great sun, Fate,   21.I feel that other coming, let it ci    <s39>
```

Figure 7. Part 2

I should turn away from it all, I want to stay here. In addition, the narrator is active as an observer to a much greater extent. In Part 1 he comments, defeated, *I'll describe it, no, I can't.* By contrast, in Part 2 he *sees, listens, hears, wonders, answers, feels.* There are, of course, negatives, but these do not determine the tone in the way in which they did in Part 1 and which they do to a large extent in Part 3, to which we now turn.

In Part 3, the processes are balanced between the physical and mental, the positive and the negative. Although we find the same set of core verbs (*go, do stay, be*) which are used throughout the story, we also find a new wider set of verbal and mental processes (*see, complain, follow, understand, presume, know, try, remember*). These observations and memories lead to the moving and humorous s51, which comes just before the long sentence that marks the end of this section and the beginning of the final part of the story. s51 stands in strong contrast with the rest of the story with its physical immediacy (*I feel the wet*

PART 3

```
o, there's no more to see,   I've seen it all, till my eyes are   <s41>
t must go their ways, that   I let go their ways and drag me he   <s41>
 me to come. <42> And what   I'm doing, all important, breathin   <s42>
ng, with words like smoke,   I can't go, I can't stay, let's se   <s42>
ds like smoke, I can't go,   I can't stay, let's see what happe   <s42>
 of sensation? <44> My God   I can't complain, it's himself all   <s44>
e warmth, less the drowse,   I can follow them well, all the vo   <s44>
 me, the wet too, at least   I presume so, I'm far. <45> My rhe   <s44>
oo, at least I presume so,   I'm far. <45> My rheumatism in any   <s44>
ps it's carrion time. <47>   I'm up there and I'm down here, un   <s47>
ime. <47> I'm up there and   I'm down here, under my gaze, foun   <s47>
night, the mist will dear,   I know my mist, for all my distrac   <s49>
 I only had been here, now   I only had been here, now I'm here   <s50>
, now I'm here still, soon   I'm here still, soon I won't be he   <s50>
n by the wood, it's larch,   I won't be here yet, toiling up th   <s50>
I don't try to understand,   I don't try to understand, I'll ne   <s50>
 you think, for the moment   I'll never try to understand any m   <s50>
ave been, always shall be,   I'm here, always have been, always   <s50>
re, they are not big. <51>   I won't be afraid of the big words   <s50>
> I don't remember coming,   I don't remember coming, I can't g   <s51>
ny, my eyes are closed and   I can't go, all my little company,   <s51>
he wind has swept it away,   I feel the wet humus harsh against   <s51>
                             I was attached to it. <52> Sometim   <s51>
```

Figure 8. Part 3

#51	I don't remember coming, I can't go, all my little company, my eyes are	46
	closed and I feel the wet humus harsh against my cheek, my hat is gone,	
	it can't be gone far, or the wind has swept it away, I was attached to it.	

Figure 9. Line 51

humus harsh against my cheek) and its dry, breathless joke (*. . .my hat is gone, it can't be gone far, or the wind has swept it away, I was attached to it*).

Part 4, in its turn, stands in marked contrast with Part 1 – and the rest of the text – having no negative forms associated with verbs for which "I" is the subject, the strongest explanation yet for the intuition of the shift from negative to positive, dark to light, which was the starting point of this analysis.

In a very short space we have travelled from the despair of the opening line of the story: *I couldn't any more, I couldn't go on* to the apparent reconciliation and harmony of : *I'm in my arms, I'm holding myself in my arms, without much tenderness, but faithfully, faithfully*. And this is a preparation for the closing exhortation:

> Sleep now, as under that ancient lamp, all twined together, tired out with so
> much talking, so much listening, so much toil and play.

```
PART 4
forest, the city, the plain too,  I've flirted with the plain too, I'  <s52>
I've flirted with the plain too,  I've given myself up for dead all o  <s52>
  jumped into the sea, that's all  I remember, a knife between his tee  <s54>
e done and came back, that's all  I remember this evening, it ended h  <s54>
  comedy, for children. <55> Yes,  I was my father and I was my son, I  <s55>
n. <55> Yes, I was my father and  I was my son, I asked myself questi  <s55>
  was my father and I was my son,  I asked myself questions and answer  <s55>
f questions and answered as best  I could, I had it told to me evenin  <s55>
ns and answered as best I could,  I had it told to me evening after e  <s55>
fter evening, the same old story  I knew by heart and couldn't believ  <s55>
n in each other. <56> That's how  I've held out till now. <57> And th  <s56>
ng again it seems to be working,  I'm in my arms, I'm holding myself   <s57>
s to be working, I'm in my arms,  I'm holding myself in my arms, with  <s57>
```

Figure 10. Part 4

But can you count on it?

At the beginning of this chapter we outlined a set of responses that one of us had had on reading *Texts for Nothing, 1,* and which we hoped to test. We feel that a computer assisted analysis has made it possible for us to develop an analysis which has given insights into our processes as readers – and which would have been difficult to undertake without such resources. The analysis demonstrates that there *is* a significant transition in the rhetorical structure of the text around sentence #52, and that this turning point in the structure appears to have its analogues in the overall structuration of the text. What has also been hinted at in the analysis is that although there is an apparent movement from alienation to integration through the course of the story, there is also something uncertain about this. In the last part of this chapter, we would like to consider the extent to which our interpretation is perhaps the result of wishful thinking on the part of an ever hopeful reader – not the conclusion one is guided towards as a response to specific wording.

The problem with *Texts for Nothing, 1* appears to be that it plays a game of hide-and-seek with the reader. Although the end of the story seems to imply a reintegration, a reestablishment of community, the text has previously created deep uncertainty about the value of any statement the writer/speaker makes – so can we believe the happy ending? After all, the text opens with a whole series of contradictions:

> Suddenly, no, at last, long last, I couldn't any more, I couldn't go on.

and continues in the same vein. Any assertion seems to be immediately negated – leaving us with the feeling that the text really is "for nothing".

Again, Wordsmith Tools can help us reveal this tendency. By using the clause boundary marker "comma" as the search string in the concordancer, it is possible to show very clearly the extent to which almost every assertion made in the text is (as in the example below) immediately countermanded, mocked, made comic:

> Glorious prospect, *but for the mist that blotted out everything,*
> *valleys, loughs, plain and sea.*

The commas do not only mark pauses for breath, they also reminding us that what has just been presented as something sure and solid is about to be whipped from under our feet.

A selection of concordance lines tells the story (Figure 11).

```
          Suddenly, no, at last, long last,  I couldn't any more
                    I'll describe the place,  that's unimportant
          The top, very flat, of a mountain,  no, a hill, but so wild,
                        Glorious prospect,  but for the mist that blot
                        How can I go on,  I shouldn't have begun, no, I
          on, I shouldn't have begun, no,  I had to begin
    have stayed in my den, snug and dry,  I couldn't
              My den, I'll describe it, no.  I can't
      I am far from all that wrangle,  I shouldn't bother with it,
    But for the mist, with good eyes,  with a telescope, I could see it from
                  I had heard tell,  I must have heard tell of the
        pity, I wouldn't see their faces,  their legs perhaps, plunged
      away from harm, the harm is done,  one day the harm was done, the
                  To change, to see,  no, there's no more to see, I've see
      see, no, there's no more to see,  I've seen it all, till my eyes
    ed me out that must go their ways,  that I let go their ways and
        breathing in and out and saying,  with words like smoke, I can
      and saying, with words like smoke,  I can't go, I can't stay, let
        smoke, I can't go, I can't stay,  let's see what happens next
```

Figure 11. Contradictions

Such a pattern of disappointed expectations has been established that how-ever sure and firm the reconciliation at the end of the text may seem, with its apparent bed-time harmony:

> Meet now, as under that ancient lamp, all twined together, tired out with so
> much talking, so much listening, so much toil and play.

. . . if we are realistic, we are also left with the thought that maybe:

> . . .this is the same old story, I knew by, heart and couldn't believe.

Conclusion

The unreliability of the text we have been discussing, should not, however, lead us to feel that the way we have analysed it has been unreliable. In fact, the Beckett story offers a salutary lesson to all of us who would attempt to adduce evidence from texts to support our readings. In short, while it is fairly obvious that you can always *prove* something by hunting around in a text to for evidence to support your argument (the practice of rogues and scoundrels since time immemorial) we hope that what we have demonstrated here is subtly different.

First, we had no idea that sentence length was going to be significant in this particular analysis. Second, we had no idea where analysis of the keyword "I" would lead us. Certainly, we have approached the text with specific purposes – both as readers and text analysis. However, we hope we have demonstrated that a bottom up approach such as the one adopted here can enrich an analysis and help us to avoid early or convenient closures in the accounts we offer of what is happening in a text..

What we have in fact been doing with our literary text is to draw on an experience of non-literary textual analysis and to use lessons learned in another arena to inform our account of this short short story. The approach we have used is related to frameworks for text analysis which have been developed for genre studies. An example is given in Figure 12 below.

Clearly, in the context of literary studies, where the focus of concern is on representational rather than referential texts (Widdowson 2004: 135), the contextual analysis stages of the framework may have little value. However, the last three stages in the Linguistic Analysis section are most decidedly relevant to our purposes. As Leech and Short did in 1981, but now with the power of modern computing at our disposal, we have been able to undertake a systematic analysis of the formal features of a literary text in order to identify features which appear to be prominent in relation to internal or external norms. In this instance, sentence length was an aspect of the *text relations / text patterning* referred to in item 9 of the genre analysis framework presented above, and was clearly a matter of prominence in relation to internal norms – very long sentences sticking out when compared with the rest of the text. Keyword analysis, by contrast, drew on the patterning of another world of texts to set a norm and then compared the Beckett text against this population. An external norm was fixed and the keyword "I" was shown to be prominent. From here, an analysis was undertaken which tested a reading of the text, and demonstrated how there were features of the text that could contribute to such a reading.

CONTEXTUAL

Analysis

1.	*name*	What is the name of the genre of which this text is an exemplar?
2.	*social context*	In what social setting is this kind of text typically produced? What constraints and obligations does this setting impose on writers and readers?
3.	*communicative purpose*	What is the communicative purpose of this text?
4.	*roles*	What roles may be required of writers and readers in this genre?
5.	*cultural values*	What shared cultural values may be required of writers and readers in this genre?
6.	*text context*	What knowledge of other texts may be required of writers and readers in this genre?
7.	*formal text features*	What shared knowledge of formal text features (conventions) is required to write effectively into this genre?

LINGUISTIC

Analysis

8.	*lexico-grammatical features*	What lexico-grammatical features of the text are statistically prominent and stylistically salient?
9.	*text relations / textual patterning*	Can textual patterns be identified in the text? What is the reason for such textual patterning?
10.	*text structure*	How is the text organised as a series of units of meaning? What is the reason for this organisation?

Figure 12. Tribble (2002: 133)

We also found during our intensive, machine assisted reading, that the text was more slippery than we had originally assumed, and that there was another patterning in play which subverted our initial reading. And again, the corpus tools were at hand to help us reconstruct the text so that clause boundaries could be brought into focus and the fundamental contradictoriness of the text be revealed. In other words, although we could not count on the text, the counting itself was an essential means for demonstrating its unreliability.

References

Aitchison, J. (2003). *Words in the Mind: An introduction to the mental lexicon* (3rd edition). Oxford: Blackwells.

Andor, J. (1989). Strategies, tactics and realistic methods of text analysis. In W. Heydrich, F. Neubauer, J. Petöfi, & E. Sözer (Eds.), *Connexity and Coherence: Analysis of text and discourse* (pp. 28–36). Berlin: Walter de Gruyter.

Aston, G. & Burnard, L. (1998). *The BNC Handbook*. Edinburgh: Edinburgh University Press.

Ball, P. (2005). A new kind of alchemy. *New Scientist*, No. 2495, 30–33, 16 April.

Barábasi, A.-L. (2002). *Linked: The new science of networks*. Cambridge, MA: Perseus.

Banerjee, S. & Pedersen, T. (2003). The design, implementation, and use of the Ngram Statistics Package. In A. F. Gelbukh (Ed.), *The Proceedings of the Fourth International Conference on Intelligent Text Processing and Computational Linguistics* February 17–21, 2003, Mexico City.

Bazerman, C. (1994). *Constructing Experience*. Carbondale, IL: Southern Illinois University Press.

de Beaugrande, R. (1980). *Text, Discourse, and Process*. London: Longman.

Beckett, S. (1967). *No's Knife: Collected shorter prose, 1947–1966*. London: Calder and Boyars.

Bell, A. (1999). News stories as narratives. In A. Jaworski & N. Coupland (Eds.), *The Discourse Reader*. London: Routledge.

Berber Sardinha, A. P. (2004). *Lingüística de Corpus*. Barueri SP, Brazil: Manole.

Biber, D. (1990). Methodological issues regarding corpus based analyses of linguistic variation. *Literary and Linguistic Computing, 5*(4), 257–269.

Biber, D. & Conrad, S. (1999). Lexical bundles in conversation and academic prose. In H. Hasselgard & S. Oksefjell (Eds.), *Out of Corpora: Studies in honor of Stig Johansson* (pp. 181–189). Amsterdam: Rodopi.

Biber, D. (1988). *Variations across Speech and Writing*. Cambridge: CUP.

Biber, D., Johansson, S., Leech, G., Conrad, S., & Finegan, E. (2000). *Longman Grammar of Spoken and Written English*. Harlow: Addison Wesley Longman.

Blake, N. F. (2002). *A Grammar of Shakespeare's Language*. Basingstoke: Palgrave.

Buchanan, M. (2002). *Small World: Uncovering nature's networks*. London: Weidenfeld & Nicholson.

Burnard, L. (2003). *BNC-baby*. Oxford: Oxford University Computer Services.

Charolles, M. (1989). Comments on Eikmeyer's and Andor's report. In W. Heydrich, F. Neubauer, J. Petöfi, & E. Sözer (Eds.), *Connexity and Coherence: Analysis of text and discourse* (pp. 37–40). Berlin: Walter de Gruyter.

Chatman, S. (1971). *Literary Style: A symposium*. Oxford: OUP.

Cortes, V. (2004). Lexical bundles in published and student disciplinary writing: Examples from history and biology. *English for Specific Purposes, 23*, 397–423.

Cowie, A. P. (Ed.). (2001). *Phraseology: Theory, analysis, and applications*. Oxford: OUP.

Coxhead, A. (2000). A new academic word list. *TESOL Quarterly, 34*(2), 213–238.

Cruse, D. A. (1986). *Lexical Semantics*. Cambridge: CUP.

Crystal, D. & Crystal, B. (2002). *Shakespeare's Words*. London: Penguin.

Culpeper, J. (2002). Computers, language and characterisation: An analysis of six characters in Romeo and Juliet. In U. Melander-Marttala, C. Östman, & M. Kytö (Eds.), *Conversation in Life and in Literature* (pp. 11–30). Uppsala: Universitetstryckeriet. [Papers from the ASLA Symposium, Association Suedoise de Linguistique Appliquée (ASLA) 15].

Dudley-Evans, T. (1994). Genre analysis: An approach to text analysis for ESP. In M. Coulthard (Ed.), *Advances in Written Discourse* (pp. 219–228). London: Routledge.

Dunning, T. (1993). Accurate methods for the statistics of surprise and coincidence. *Computational Linguistics, 19*(1), 61–74.

Evert, S. & Krenn, B. (2005). Using small random samples for the manual evaluation of statistical association measures. *Computer Speech and Language, 19*(4), 450–466.

Fairclough, N. (1989). *Language and Power*. Harlow: Longman.

Faloutsos, M., Faloutsos, P., & Faloutsos, C. (1999). On power-law relationships of the internet topology. In *Applications, Technologies, Architectures, and Protocols for Computer Communication. Proceedings of the conference on applications, technologies, architectures, and protocols for computer communication* (pp. 251–262). Cambridge, MA: ACM Press.

Flowerdew, J. (1993). An educational or process approach to the teaching of professional genres. *ELT Journal, 47*(4), 305–316.

Fowler, R. (1991). *Language in the News*. London: Routledge.

Francis, G., Hunston, S., & Manning, E. (Eds.). (1996). *Grammar Patterns 1: Verbs*. London: HarperCollins.

Granger, S. & Tribble, C. (1998). Exploiting learner corpus data in the classroom: Form-focused instruction and data-driven learning. In S. Granger (Ed.), *Learner Language on Computer*. Harlow: Longman.

Halliday, M. A. K. (1973). *Explorations in the Functions of Language*. London: Edward Arnold.

Halliday, M. A. K. (1989). *Spoken and Written Language*. Oxford: OUP.

Halliday, M. A. K. (1994). *An Introduction to Functional Grammar* (2nd edition). London: Edward Arnold.

Hoey, M. & Winter, E. (1986). Clause relations and the writer's communicative purpose. In B. Couture (Ed.), *Functional Approaches to Writing* (pp. 120–141). London: Frances Pinter.

Hoey, M. (1983). *On the Surface of Discourse*. London: George Allen and Unwin.

Hoey, M. (1991). *Patterns of Lexis in Text*. Oxford: OUP.

Hoey, M. (1997). From concordance to text structure: New uses for computer corpora. In J. Melia & B. Lewandoska (Eds.), *PALC 97: Practical applications in language corpora* (pp. 106–118). Lodz: Lodz University Press.

Hoey, M. (2004). Lexical priming and the properties of text. In A. Partington, J. Morley, & L. Haarman (Eds.), *Corpora and Discourse* (pp. 385–412). Bern: Peter Lang.

Hoey, M. (2005). *Lexical Priming: A new theory of words and language.* London: Routledge.

Hope, J. (2003). *Shakespeare's Grammar.* London: The Arden Shakespeare.

Howarth, P. (1996). *Phraseology in English Academic Writing.* Tübingen: Niemeyer.

Jones, K. S. (1971). *Automatic Keyword Classification for Information Retrieval.* London: Butterworths.

Jordan, R. R. (1997). *English for Academic Purposes.* Cambridge: CUP.

Katz, S. (1996). Distribution of common words and phrases in text and language modelling. *Natural Language Engineering, 2*(1), 15–59.

Kintsch, W. & van Dijk, T. (1978). Toward a model of text comprehension and production. *Psychological Review, 85*(5), 363–394.

Krishnamurthy, R. (2004). *English Collocation Studies: The OSTI report.* London: Continuum.

Lee, D. (2001). Genres, registers, text types, domains and styles: Clarifying the concepts and navigating a path through the BNC jungle. *Language Learning & Technology,* Special issue on *Using Corpora in Language Teaching and Learning, 5*(3), 37–72.

Lee, D. (2003). *BNC Index.* URL: http://clix.to/davidlee00, last accessed 2003–12–11.

Leech, G. & Short, M. (1981). *Style in Fiction.* Harlow: Longman.

Leech, G. N. (1969). *A linguistic guide to English poetry.* Longman: Harlow.

Louw, B. (1993). The diagnostic potential of semantic prosodies. In M. Baker, G. Francis, & E. Tognini-Bonelli (Eds.), *Text and Technology: In honour of John Sinclair* (pp. 157–176). Amsterdam: John Benjamins.

McCarthy, M. (1990). *Vocabulary.* Oxford: OUP.

Nation, P. (1990). *Teaching & Learning Vocabulary.* New York: Newbury House.

Nelson, M. (2000). A Corpus-Based Study of Business English and Business English Teaching Materials. PhD Thesis, University of Manchester.

Oakes, M. (1998). *Statistics for Corpus Linguistics.* Edinburgh: Edinburgh University Press.

Phillips, M. (1989). *Lexical Structure of Text* [Discourse analysis monographs 12]. Birmingham: University of Birmingham.

Pustet, R. (2004). Zipf and his heirs. *Language Sciences, 26,* 1–25.

Richards, J., Platt, J., & Weber, H. (Eds.). (1985). *Longman Dictionary of Applied Linguistics.* London: Longman.

Rossner, R. & Widdowson, H. G. (1983). Talking Shop: H. G. Widdowson on literature and ELT. *ELT Journal, 37*(1).

Rundell, M. (Ed.). (2002). *Macmillan English dictionary for advanced learners.* Oxford: Macmillan.

Savický, P. & Hlaváčová, J. (2002). Measures of word commonness. *Journal of Quantitative Linguistics, 9*(3), 215–231.

Scott, M. (1996a). *WordSmith Tools.* Oxford: OUP.

Scott, M. (1996b). *WordSmith Tools Manual.* Oxford: OUP.

Scott, M. (1997a). PC Analysis of key words – and key key words. *System, 25*(1), 1–13.

Scott, M. (1997b). The right word in the right place: Key word associates in two languages. *AAA – Arbeiten aus Anglistik und Amerikanistik, 22*(2), 239–252.

Scott, M. (1999). *WordSmith Tools Users Help File*. Oxford: OUP.

Scott, M. (2002). Picturing the key words of a very large corpus and their lexical upshots – or getting at the Guardian's view of the world. In B. Kettemann & G. Marko (Eds.), *Teaching and Learning by Doing Corpus Analysis* (pp. 43–50). Amsterdam: Rodopi.

Sigurd, B., Eeg-Olofsson, M., & van de Weijer, J. (2004). Word length, sentence length and frequency – Zipf revisited. *Studia Linguistica, 58*(1), 37–52.

Sinclair, J. McH. (Ed.). (1987). *Collins COBUILD English Language Dictionary*. London: Collins.

Sinclair, J. McH. (Ed.). (1990). *Collins Cobuild English Grammar*. London: Collins.

Sinclair, J. McH. (1991). *Corpus, Concordance, Collocation*. Oxford: OUP.

Sinclair, J. McH. (2003). *Reading Concordances*. London: Longman.

Sinclair, J. McH. (2004). *Trust the Text: Language corpus and discourse*. London: Routledge.

Sinclair, J. McH., Jones, S., & Daley, R. (1969). Report to OSTI on Project C/LP/08. In R. Krishnamurthy (Ed., 2004), *English Collocation Studies: The OSTI report*. London: Continuum.

Sinclair, J. McH. & Coulthard, M. (1975). *Towards an Analysis of Discourse*. Oxford: OUP.

Stubbs, M. (1996). *Text and Corpus Analysis*. Oxford: Blackwell.

Stubbs, M. (2002). *Words and Phrases: Corpus studies of lexical semantics*. Oxford: Blackwell.

Summers, D. (Ed.). (1987). *Longman Dictionary of Contemporary English*. Harlow: Longman.

Swales, J. M. (1981). *Aspects of Articles Introductions* [Aston ESP Research Reports No. 1]. Birmingham: University of Aston.

Swales, J. M. (1990). *Genre Analysis*. Cambridge: CUP.

Tribble, C. (1996). Feature review: WordSmith Tools Call review, September, 13–18.

Tribble, C. (2002). Corpora and corpus analysis: New windows on academic writing. In J. Flowerdew (Ed.), *Academic Discourse*. Harlow: Addison Wesley Longman.

Widdowson, H. G. (1975). *Stylistics and the Teaching of Literature*. Oxford: OUP.

Widdowson, H. G. (1992). *Practical Stylistics*. Oxford: OUP.

Widdowson, H. G. (2004). *Text, Context, Pretext*. Oxford: Blackwell.

Williams, R. (1983). *Keywords* (2nd edition). London: Fontana.

Winter, E. O. (1977). A clause relational approach to English texts: A study of some predictive lexical items in written discourse. *Instructional Science, 6*(1), 1–92.

Zipf, G. K. (1965). *Human Behavior and the Principle of Least Effort*. New York: Hafner. (Facsimile of 1949 edition).

Name index

Subject index

In the series *Studies in Corpus Linguistics (SCL)* the following titles have been published thus far or are scheduled for publication: